FOUNDATION

Business

Hala Seliet

HEINEMANN GNVQ

FOUNDATION

Business

Hala Seliet

Edexcel
Success through qualifications

Heinemann Educational Publishers,
Halley Court, Jordan Hill, Oxford OX2 8EJ
A division of Reed Educational & Professional Publishing Ltd

Heinemann is a registered trademark of Reed Educational & Professional Publishing Limited

OXFORD MELBOURNE AUCKLAND JOHANNESBURG BLANTYRE GABORONE
IBADAN PORTSMOUTH NH (USA) CHICAGO

First published 2000
2004 2003 2002 2001 2000
10 9 8 7 6 5 4 3 2 1

A catalogue record for this book is available from the British Library on request.

ISBN 0 435 45305 X

Typeset by TechType, Abingdon, Oxfordshire

Printed and bound in Great Britain by The Bath Press Ltd., Bath

Tel: 01865 888058 www.heinemann.co.uk

Contents

Acknowledgements

The author and publishers would like to thank the following individuals and organisations for permission to reproduce photographs and other copyright material:

p. 3 The Body Shop; p. 8, 20, 24, 27, 30, 42, 46, 50, 79, 91, 109, 141, 142 Photodisc; p. 14, 94 McDonald's; p. 31, 77 Sally & Richard Greenhill; p. 43 Focus Do It All; p. 45 Customer Services Department, Heinemann; p. 47 Alliance & Leicester; p. 62 River Island; p. 63 Joseph Dobson & Sons Ltd; p. 64 Halifax PLC; p. 67 Co-Operative Wholesale Society (CWS); p. 71, 76 Corbis; p. 74, 87 Boots PLC; p. 75 Northern Foods PLC; p. 83 Meadowhall, Sheffield; p. 102 Tony Stone.

Every effort has been made to contact the copyright holders of material published in this book. We would be glad to hear from unacknowledged sources at the first opportunity.

Hala Seliet
August 2000

Introduction

How to use this book

This book has been written as a brand new text for students who are working to the 2000 national standards for Foundation GNVQ in Business. It covers the three compulsory units for the award.

These units are:

1 How a business works
2 Investigating business
3 Finance in business.

Within each unit, the text is organised under chapters and headings which closely match the headings in the GNVQ units, making it easy for you to find your way around the unit.

By working through the units, you will find all the knowledge and ideas you need to prepare your assessment.

Assessment

Assessment in the new GNVQ is carried out on the whole unit, rather than by many smaller pieces of work. The methods of assessment are:

- one major assignment, for example, carrying out an investigation into the features of two different kinds of businesses
- an external test, set and marked by the awarding body, for example, Edexcel.

At the end of units 1 and 2, you will find a unit assessment section which provides you with practice for both forms of assignment. At the end of each unit in the book, you will find a short unit test. This can be used to check your knowledge of the unit and also to prepare for the external test.

Special features of the book

Throughout the text there are a number of features which are designed to encourage discussion and group work, and to help you relate the theory to real work in business.

Activity: Activities that encourage you to apply the theory to a practical situation

Did you know?:   Interesting facts and snippets of information about business.

Case studies: Examples of real (or simulated) situations in business. Questions on the case studies will enable you to explore the key issues and deepen your understanding of the subject.

Key Terms: Throughout the text, you will find sections containing definitions of important or new terms that you have come across in that chapter. These are a useful reference source, and they will help you reinforce what you have learnt.

Other features included at the end of the book are: **Blank documents for photocopying** – in Unit 3, there are lots of opportunities for you to practise filling in the financial documents that are used in business, and your tutor will photocopy the blank forms for you to use; and a useful **Index**.

Related titles for Foundation GNVQ in Business:

Student book with Edexcel options (0435452975)

Tutor Resource Pack (0435452983)

How a business works

In this unit you will look at a business to find out how it operates. You will find out about:

- what your chosen business does
- how businesses are structured
- how businesses are divided into functional areas
- how businesses look after customers
- how businesses communicate with customers and employees.

During your study of the unit, you will need to collect information about a business of your choice so that you can produce an illustrated case study. This must demonstrate that you understand why the business operates, how it is organised and the type of functional areas within it (one of which must be explained in detail). You also need to demonstrate your understanding of what customer service is, along with a clear knowledge of communication methods within your chosen business.

Chapter I An introduction to business

What businesses do

All businesses have a main activity which involves producing goods, providing a service, or both. You will need to find out the main activity of a business and understand what it is aiming to do.

ACTIVITY

1 What is the main activity of a hairdressing salon?
2 What is the main activity of a supermarket?
3 What is the main activity of your favourite clothes shop?

How businesses are structured

The structure of a business means the way in which activities are arranged by putting people who do similar work together, so they can communicate effectively and the work can be divided between them efficiently.

Organisation charts

The structure of a business can be illustrated in an organisation chart. Page 4 shows an organisation chart for a manufacturing business. An organisation chart usually shows the job titles of employees and their relationships with each other. Sometimes the job-holder's name is shown. An organisation chart can benefit a business in a number of ways by showing:

1 different functional areas
2 job titles and job roles
3 how many staff are under a particular manager's control
4 lines of decision-making and levels of responsibility
5 potential communication problems
6 opportunities for promotion
7 new employees where they fit into the overall organisation.

Major roles in an organisation are usually those of directors, managers, supervisors and team members. The organisation chart on page 4 illustrates this:

CASE STUDY – Boots' business objectives

The Boots Company operates in the retailing, manufacturing and marketing of health and personal care products throughout the world.

Boots' main aim is to make a good profit. It will do this by investing in the business and making sure that people who have invested in the company (shareholders) get a fair reward. However, the company also wants to make sure it has a good business reputation as a well-managed, ethical and socially responsible company.

With your tutor, read the case study carefully and answer the following questions:

1 What is Boots' main aim?
2 Why does Boots look after shareholders' interests?
3 What other aims does the business have?
4 What does "socially responsible company" mean?

CASE STUDY – The Body Shop
and environmental commitment

In 1976, Anita Roddick opened the first Body Shop in Brighton. It sold 25 skin and hair care products. Body Shop International PLC now has over 1500 shops in 47 countries selling over 400 different products. However, Body Shop does not just make and sell toiletries and cosmetics. The organisation campaigns on issues relating to human rights, and animal and environmental protection. This has included campaigning for women's rights and against nuclear testing.

The Body Shop's main business aim is to make social and environmental changes happen. Businesses need to make a profit to survive. The emphasis at Body Shop is on profit with a social responsibility, i.e. "profit with principle". As a public limited company, the legal owners of The Body Shop are shareholders. Although shareholders may recognise the value of campaigning on social and environmental issues, the share price remains important.

Read the above case study carefully and answer the following questions:

1 What is The Body Shop's main business objective?
2 Who are the owners of The Body Shop?
3 What is the shareholders' main objective?
4 How do you think The Body Shop management tries to satisfy their shareholders?

Chairperson

He or she will chair the board meetings and have significant influence in the appointment of the managing director.

Board of directors

Members of the board of directors are the representatives of the shareholders (the owners). Their role is to deal with major policy matters such as decisions on capital investment. The directors have a responsibility to act in the interests of the company. They are also normally shareholders in the company.

Managing Director

As the name suggests, he or she is an executive director who takes the leading role in the day-to-day running of the company. He or she will be supported by a number of specialist managers.

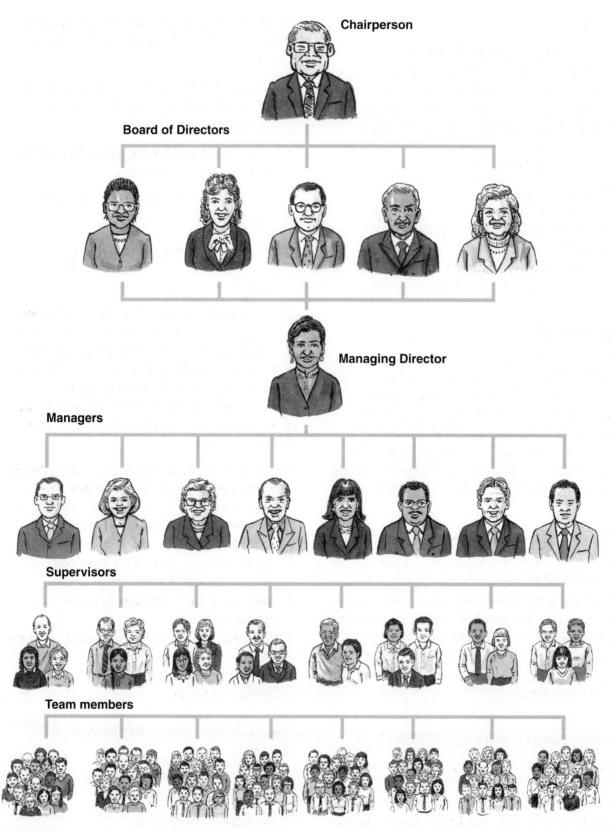

Chairperson

Board of Directors

Managing Director

Managers

Supervisors

Team members

An organisation chart for a manufacturing business

Managers

Senior managers may be heads of department. They may be assisted by middle or junior managers who each run their own section or unit. Some managers look after people, others look after tasks. Managers in a business are responsible for five main areas of activity:

1 decision making
2 problem solving
3 planning and setting long-term objectives
4 ensuring targets are achieved
5 organising the working environment.

Supervisors

Supervisors are responsible to the junior or middle management, and responsible for the team members. Their main tasks are to supervise the team work and make sure that daily targets are met and problems solved. A supervisor is a leader who is responsible for probably five or six people, sometimes in an individual department or section.

Production operatives

Production operatives work on the day-to-day jobs that make the business run, e.g. they will be shop assistants, operate machines in a factory, or be clerks. Their tasks involve the intake of materials, processing, production, transport and distribution of products and, often, the use of machinery or equipment to manufacture them.

Team members/Support staff

These are people who support the internal workings of the organisation and perform support tasks for managers. When you start work, your first role might be that of team member, i.e. a clerk in the wages section or an administrative assistant in a solicitor's office. The main duties of team members are to:

* carry out the duties as specified on the job description, as required by the manager or supervisor

* obey reasonable instructions (remember your legal obligations)

* co-operate with other team members.

 # ACTIVITIES

Draw an organisational chart for your school or college. The chart should show who makes the decisions in your school or college, and who carries out the instructions. Find a tutor in your school or college who has been working there for more than seven years and show him or her the current chart of your school or college.

1 Ask him or her if this chart is any different from the school or college chart seven years ago.
2 Find out who left the school or college and who joined it.
3 Find out if any new posts have been created during the past seven years.
4 Find out if there are any jobs that no longer exist.
5 Find out which tutor(s) is/are still working in the school or college.
6 Find out which tutor(s) is/are new in your school or college.

Discuss, in your groups, the following statement:

"Organisation charts quickly become out of date".

Do you agree or disagree?

CASE STUDY –
Ali, Crombie and Patel Partnership

Ali, Crombie and Patel Partnership is a dental surgery that is owned by three people who met as students at the London Dental Institute. The dental surgery employs two dental nurses, a hygienist, a receptionist, and a cleaner. The three dentists are joint managers of the business as well as its owners.

Draw an organisation or business chart for the above dental surgery – who do you think will be at the top of this chart? Who will be at the bottom of the chart?

Key Terms

Board of directors Those persons employed by the shareholders of a company. Their task is to look after the interests of the shareholders.

Chairperson The person elected by the shareholders to oversee the decisions made by the Board of Directors and ensure the company achieves its aims.

Managing Director The person appointed by the Board of Directors to be responsible for the management team that runs the company on a day-to-day basis.

Organisation chart A chart that illustrates the job titles of employees and their relationships with each other in a business.

Shareholders These are the people who have invested money in the business and take a share in the profits. They elect the Board of Directors.

Chapter 2 How businesses are divided into functional areas

Even for small businesses with only one or two employees, different tasks must be carried out. For example, in a corner shop, the owner must divide his or her time between different tasks such as:

- serving customers
- purchasing goods
- pricing the goods
- promoting the shop (advertising)
- receiving customers' payments
- cleaning the shop
- displaying products on the shelves.

Task

What tasks will an ice cream seller do, in addition to selling ice cream?

Why different functions?

Most businesses are made up of different departments, each with their own specialised function. All these functions work together to help the business perform efficiently and achieve its objectives. The different departments usually include human resources, finance, administration, production, marketing and customer services. In this chapter you will learn about how each of these different departments is run, and you will also find out how they work together. There is a separate chapter on the customer services department (see Chapter 3).

The Human Resources function

The human resources (or personnel) department within a business is responsible for making sure that employees can work

Light Delight Ltd

To show you what people in each of the functional areas do in their jobs, this unit includes 'personal profiles' which focus on different people and their jobs. You will see that all of these people work for a made-up business called Light Delight Ltd, an ice cream manufacturing company. For example, on page 30, there is a section about Mike Johnson, the Marketing Manager for Light Delight Ltd. These profiles will help you understand what daily activities might be carried out by someone who works in each of the functional areas: human resources, finance, administration, production, marketing and sales, and customer service. You will come across the Light Delight business again in Unit 3, when you learn about financial documents.

effectively and safely. They cover the following areas:

- recruitment, retention and dismissal
- health and safety
- training, development and promotion
- maintaining staff records
- employee organisations and unions.

Recruitment, retention and dismissal
Recruitment

It is important for any business to recruit the right people. If the right people are recruited, they are likely to stay with the company. If the wrong people are recruited, they will either leave (and the company will have to go through the expensive recruitment process again) or they will stay, but do their job badly.

Any system of recruitment should have three main features:

1 be effective in choosing the right candidate
2 cheap to operate
3 fair to all candidates.

Businesses should recruit the best workforce for the job regardless of their colour, religion, disability or ethnic origin. The law requires that all companies must state in their job advertisements that they are equal opportunity employers.

The first stage of the recruitment process is to decide upon the job that needs to be done and the type of person you are looking for to do it.

Jack Evans, Human Resources (Personnel) Manager

 Jack is the Human Resources Manager at Light Delight Ltd. He is 35 years old and joined the company three years ago. After leaving school at the age of 16, Jack did a BTEC National in Business and Finance and later did an HNC including personnel management.

People are the most important resources in ensuring the successful running of a company. Jack believes that the main task of a Human Resources Manager is to help the business gain the maximum benefit from its people.

He is very keen to create a friendly and motivating business working environment. As Human Resources Manager he will play a central role in looking after the company's workforce.

Jack's main responsibilities are:

• **To look** after the welfare of the staff.

• **To select** and recruit the best workforce to work for the company.

• **To provide** adequate and effective training programmes for staff.

• **To ensure** a safe and healthy environment and to make sure that all employees understand the health and safety issues.

• **To provide** expertise and support in motivating the workforce.

• **To deal** with conflict between the management team and the workforce.

• **To take** disciplinary action if employees don't meet the required standards of conduct, attendance, time keeping and job performance.

Jack expects staff to stay in the business for an average of 2 to 3 years. He gets concerned if a member of staff leaves the business after only a few months. He believes that the recruitment, selection and training of staff is very expensive and losing them quickly means that money has been wasted.

Jack has a weekly meeting with his assistant to discuss any recent human resources, health and safety and training and development issues.

He also has a monthly meeting with the Board of Directors to report on any changes in personnel.

Job description

The job description will include an outline of the tasks that are to be carried out and the responsibilities of the person doing the job, for example:

'Come and work for the UK's premier bus company'

'Our PCV drivers receive competitive rates of pay plus benefits'

PremierBus Cardiff

PCV DRIVER

Main purpose of the job

To sell a service in the form of a bus journey to customers, satisfying their needs and encouraging them to travel again.

Main Duties

- *Greeting customers and ensuring customer satisfaction through answering customer queries, providing information on services, routes, and fares.*

- *Operating a service for customers on designated routes to a designated timetable, ensuring the safety and comfort of passengers at all times.*

- *Taking fares and issuing tickets, using computerised equipment, and checking concessionary fare tickets, multi-journey cards etc.*

- *Balancing and accounting for cash receipts taken during the course of duties, paying in cash to cash-counting machines in accordance with company procedures.*

- *Operating radio equipment in line with operational requirements.*

- *Conducting, within their expertise and training, vehicle checks and reporting any faults.*

- *Collecting information (ie witness statements) and submitting written reports regarding accidents, incidents etc, as necessary to minimise potential claims against the Company.*

Job description for PCV driver

ACTIVITIES

Read the job description for a PCV Driver at PremierBus Cardiff on page 9 and answer the following questions:

1 What do you think is the most important duty for a bus driver among those listed above? Explain your answer.
2 PremierBus is very keen to provide a high quality customer service. Find, from the job description, what supports this statement.

3 FirstBus is committed to Health and Safety issues. Find, from the job description, what supports this statement.

Person specification

Once a job description has been produced, it is possible to describe the kind of person you would want to fill that job. This involves drawing up a person specification.

ACTIVITIES

Read the person specification (left) for PCV Drivers and answer the following questions:

1 What does the person specification describe?
2 Which of the skills (in the person specification) is necessary for a bus driver to carry out each of the following duties:
   a Greeting customers and ensuring customer satisfaction through answering customer queries, providing information on services, routes, and fares.
   b Operating a service for customers on designated routes to a designated timetable, ensuring the safety and comfort of passengers at all times.
   c Taking fares and issuing tickets, using computerised equipment, and checking

---

PremierBus Cardiff

PCV DRIVER, AGE 21-60 YEARS

1 *Must be able to write legibly.*

2 *Must be able to read.*

3 *Must be able to follow verbal and written instructions.*

4 *Must be able and willing to use the telephone/radio in communication with the company.*

5 *Must be able to communicate clearly, concisely and courteously with the public, including irate and anxious passengers.*

6 *Must demonstrate some understanding of, and agreement with, the principles of Equal Opportunity.*

7 *Must be able and willing to work alone for long periods without close supervision.*

8 *Must be able to identify enquiries which can be dealt with by themselves and those which require referral.*

9 *Must be able to deal effectively with frequent interruptions and resume the task in hand without loss of efficiency.*

10 *Must be able to demonstrate a positive approach to change.*

Person specification for PCV driver job

concessionary fare tickets, multi-journey cards etc.

d Collecting information (i.e. witness statements) and submitting written reports regarding accidents, incidents etc, as necessary to minimise potential claims against the Company.

Having drawn up a job description and person specification, the human resources department advertise the job. Organisations can recruit internally or externally, i.e. they can choose people from inside the organisation or widen the field to outsiders.

Internal recruitment

This means recruiting someone who already works within the company. Methods of internal recruitment include staff notice boards and staff magazines. Recruiting from within the organisation has a number of advantages and disadvantages.

ACTIVITY

Match the following sentences under the two headings – **Advantages** and **Disadvantages** of internal recruitment:

- Appointing from within the organisation may cause jealousy and resentment among other staff, who may feel they have been "passed over" for promotion.
- There is less risk involved, because the employer already knows the person who will be filling the vacancy.
- There is no "buzz" that follows when a new person joins the organisation.
- It's cheaper because it saves the costs of advertising.
- It saves the cost of training a new employee to introduce him or her to the job.

- No new ideas are brought into the business from outside.
- The opportunity for promotion in the organisation encourages people to work hard.

External recruitment

Sometimes the management will decide to appoint someone from outside. Having decided on how widely to advertise, the company must choose the method it will use. In making this decision, the firm will have to balance the cost of advertising against the need to attract a high quality of applicants. Many employers advertise vacancies in:

- local schools and colleges
- local newspapers
- national newspapers
- job centres
- internet.

Interviews

After the human resources department has advertised the job, they will usually deal with the letters of application that the business hopes to receive from people who are interested in the job. The human resources department will often sort through the applications before passing them on to whichever manager is advertising for a new employee. The manager will look through the applications and will make a list of those people who look most suitable. The human resources department will contact these people to arrange a time when they can be interviewed. Someone from the human resources department will often help the manager to conduct the interviews. After all of the candidates have been interviewed, the manager and/or human resources department will select who they think is the best person for the job. If this person decides to take the job, it will then be up to the human resources department to sort out the details of when he or she will start the job etc.

> *BUS DRIVERS required* 需求
>
> *PremierBus Cardiff, a subsidiary of PremierBus Group PLC, is seeking to recruit high quality staff who are:* 试图 找
>
> - *smart in appearance*
> - *can work flexible hours*
> - *have an outgoing and friendly manner*
> - *enjoy driving.*
>
> *So, if you currently hold a PCV licence, or have a clean driving licence and would like to train as a bus driver, then we want to hear from you. Call in at our Macaulay Street Travel Shop for an application form.*
>
> *All application forms must be returned by Tuesday 22 December. We offer secure employment with all the expected benefits from the UK's largest bus company.*
>
> **Free travel pass *Free uniforms*

Advertising for a job vacancy at PremierBus PLC in *The Examiner* local newspaper

ACTIVITY

Read the advertisement (left) and answer the following questions:

1 What information about the job is included in the advertisement?
2 What benefits do bus drivers get from joining the company?
3 What sort of person is required for the bus driver job? Why do you think this is the case?
4 How could people who are interested apply for this job?
5 Why do you think this advertisement appeared in the local newspaper for the Cardiff area?

Staff welfare (perks and benefits)

Nowadays businesses are keen to look after the welfare of their staff in order to increase productivity. These additional services, such

CASE STUDY – Perks at PremierBus Company

PremierBus is the largest bus service company in the UK, and employees are entitled to the following perks:

- a contributory pension scheme 计划
- free uniform for staff who deal directly with customers or those whose work requires protective clothing
- free travel for the employees and his or her immediate family
- holiday pay and sickness benefit
- opportunities for career development
- employee's share scheme.

1 Why does PremierBus Company provide the above perks to employees?

2 What is the effect of the above perks on employees' motivation and attitude to work?

3 In your view, what is the most important perk which employees will benefit from?

4 Discuss in your group the following statement:

"Happy employees make happy customers".

as staff discount, the provision of a social club and private medical insurance, are called benefits or "perks".

End of employment

Employers seek to end the employment of workers for two basic reasons:

1 redundancy – where workers are not needed in the business any more (surplus to requirements)

2 dismissal for misconduct, incapacity or incompetence.

However, a major constraint on employers is the rights of employees under various Employment Protection Acts.

Redundancy

It is the situation that results when an employee's contract of employment is ended because that job no longer exists either because the company is closing down, new technology has taken over, or costs need to be cut.

Dismissal

Over the years, the rules for dismissing employees have become quite complex. The heart of the matter lies in the difference between what the courts regard to be "fair" and "unfair" dismissal.

Fair dismissal can take place when an employee can be shown to be guilty of:

a wilful destruction of company property

b sexual or racial harassment

c continuous bad timekeeping

d a negative attitude at work

e inability to do the job

f sleeping on the job.

Health and safety

Working conditions can have a direct effect on the health and safety of the people in the workplace. One of the main functions of the human resources department is to provide the best possible working conditions for employees, and to ensure that they work in a healthy and safe environment.

Nowadays, increasing attention is paid to certain safety hazards that have previously been ignored. "Sick building syndrome" is a term used to describe buildings that are thought to cause illness amongst staff. Possible causes could be:

- poor air conditioning

- poor ventilation

- dust from carpets and furnishings

- ineffective lighting.

There is also concern that staff who operate computer equipment for long periods of time may suffer from eye strain, tiredness or stress. Another, increasing, threat to staff, particularly those who deal with the general public or work in areas which are open to general public, is violence. Many employers now make sure that the work environment is made as safe as possible by:

- improving communications systems (installing panic buttons)

- installing glass screens in reception areas

- reorganising work schedules so that no one has to be alone in a high risk area.

Health and Safety at Work Act, 1974 (HASAWA)

The health and safety of employees is a major aspect of working conditions. The duty of employers to provide safe working conditions is often backed up by statutory (legal) requirements. The Health and Safety Act sets out the duties of both the employer and the employee relating to health and safety (*contd. on page 15*):

CASE STUDY – Health and safety at McDonald's

All McDonald's restaurants comply with the Building and Health and Safety regulations. A safety management and training system ensures that employees at all levels have all necessary knowledge of the policies and procedures to protect the safety of customers, fellow employees and themselves. McDonald's commitment to safety is ongoing, with a system designed to allow continuous improvement. The company views compliance with legislation as a minimum requirement, and aims for the highest standards of health and safety. The company has a National Safety Manager and seven Regional Hygiene and Safety Advisors.

Health and Safety training for all staff is a priority. All food preparation and service staff, and all dining area staff, receive safety training before they start work for McDonald's, with ongoing training throughout their employment. All management staff complete additional safety training, with a dedicated health and safety training course. Managers also receive training to become qualified first aiders. There will always be at least one qualified first aider in duty at any time. A more advanced safety course is provided for the Restaurant Manager and Regional Training Officers.

Source: Educational Package (McDonald's)

Read the above case study carefully and answer the following questions:

1 Why do you think Health and Safety is important for McDonald's customers?

2 Why do staff at McDonald's receive Health and Safety training? How will the business benefit from this training?

3 Why do you think Assistant Managers and Regional Training officers at McDonald's receive more Health and Safety training than Restaurant Managers?

4 Dining Area staff receive specific Health and Safety training. Why do you think this is the case?

The employers' main duty or responsibility is to provide a safe workplace, including arrangements for hazards such as fire, and the maintenance and safety of machinery and equipment.

Employees have the duty to take reasonable care for the safety of themselves and other working colleagues at all times, and to co-operate with the employer on all matters of safety.

 **ACTIVITY**

Find out about the Health and Safety regulations in your school or college. Ask your tutor about regulations for fire practice and emergency situations.

Employers' obligations for Health and Safety

Every employer should produce a written statement of the organisation's Health and Safety policy together with details of the arrangements for carrying out that policy. A health and safety policy should include details of:

- how accidents should be reported
- those who are trained in first aid
- those who are safety representatives (and the duties they must undertake)
- the person responsible overall for the Health and Safety policy
- safe working practices.

Safe working practices can be divided into:

- good housekeeping
- the provision of suitable equipment and training in the use of it
- the provision of suitable furniture and proper care and use of it

- suitable accommodation
- reduction in noise
- safe working habits
- provision of information.

Employees' obligations to health and safety

Although your employer cannot delegate his or her responsibility for health, safety and welfare, you must remember that under the Health and Safety at Work Act you also have an obligation to make sure that you:

- take care of your health and safety
- take reasonable care of the health and safety of other people who may be injured by your careless actions
- co-operate with your employer or any other person carrying out the duties under the Act.

Training

Training is all activities involved in teaching someone the skills, attitude and knowledge required for a job. It involves guiding or teaching people to do something by providing them with a planned programme of exercises and activities. Training should involve workers before they actually start the job, during the first few weeks of employment (induction) and throughout their careers.

Benefits of training

Training develops the skills and knowledge of employees to help them to do their jobs better, and prepares them for more demanding jobs in the future. It should be a rewarding process. If employees can do their jobs well, they will feel confident in their abilities and enjoy their work more. This leads to greater job satisfaction.

Training benefits those being trained and the organisations for whom they work. Training can therefore be one of the most effective ways for a business to add value.

Benefits to individuals include:

- greater skills
- more knowledge
- more confidence
- better career prospects
- better opportunities for promotion.

Benefits to the business include:

- more motivated and productive employees
- better quality work
- more job satisfaction
- greater ability to use the latest technology
- easier to achieve business objectives.

Staff development and promotion

Staff development is slightly different from training. It is concerned with identifying the abilities of employees and providing them with training opportunities that will prepare them for promotion, e.g. staff development programmes in River Island and Marks & Spencer.

Staff appraisal interviews

Training is not the only way of improving the performance of staff. Some organisations use a system of appraisal for staff development. This means that the employee's standards of work are discussed and assessed by the employee and his or her manager. It is usual for the manager to write a report of the discussion. Sometimes the report is read by the employee, who checks that it is an accurate record of what was discussed.

An appraisal system helps to identify a person's areas of strength and weaknesses at work. If weaknesses are identified, appropriate training can be offered to help the worker improve in his or her job. This benefits the firm, by increasing labour productivity and efficiency, and the employee, by providing him or her with opportunities for promotion. In some large organisations the appraisal report will be taken into account when considering employees for promotion or salary increases.

Some businesses are also quite keen to have constant contact with employees by holding staff interviews. For example the management in River Island finds out staff views and training needs in appraisal interviews every year. The interviews offer an ideal opportunity to discuss any problem staff might have. If members of staff are unhappy they will not perform to the best of their abilities.

Other forms of staff development

There are other ways which large businesses use to develop staff skills, and experience which offer them wider opportunities for career progress and promotion. For example:

Job rotation: changing jobs at regular intervals. This makes the job less boring and provides staff with new experience in different areas of the business. For example, bank staff are usually rotated between different departments such as saving or current accounts.

Job enrichment: gives greater responsibilities to the person who is doing the job to provide him or her with a sense of achievement. For example, a car designer could be given the opportunity to create new ideas and design.

Job enlargement: makes the job as big as possible by adding more tasks and responsibilities, but without sense of achievement e.g. bus driver giving him more responsibilities to maintain and clean the bus.

Working hours

Flex-Time System: flexible working time (FWT) is increasingly used in the modern workplace. At 'peak' times all members of staff will be at work. Outside these 'core' hours, there is more flexibility and staff have a certain amount of choice about when they work, provided they work a minimum number of hours.

ACTIVITY

Find a member of your family, a relative or a friend who benefits from the flexible time system. Ask them about the advantages and drawback of this system.

Shift work: in many industries it is important to have machinery working all the time in order to make the most efficient and profitable use of resources. This is true of industries such as textiles, chemicals, steel coal mining, food processing and many others.

Staff records

The human resources department will keep a record of every employee, past and present. This is usually kept on a computer database. The record will include details of the employee's name and address, date of birth, current job title and salary, starting and leaving date, qualifications and experience and payroll number. There is usually a place for the personnel section to record additional training courses and qualifications that are obtained.

Employees' organisations

One of the main functions of the human resources department is to resolve conflicts between management and staff in order to create stability and ensure the smooth running of the business.

These days employees take a more active role in a business. Management is generally keen to inform, consult or involve employees in decision making through different channels of communication.

In a small business, each employee is probably able to negotiate with management on his or her own behalf. In medium and large businesses, however, it is not possible for each employee to deal directly with management. Therefore, the employees usually elect a body, such as a staff association or works council, to represent them. A staff association provides a meeting ground for employees and employer. Sometimes it is also involved in management decision making. In industries with a recognised trade union, it is often the trade union which negotiates with the employer on behalf of the employee.

Trade unions

A trade union is an organisation that represents employees at work. The Employment Act gives employees the right to either join or not join a trade union. Whether or not an employer must recognise a trade union is being debated at the moment. The law will be changed in the near future.

Trade unions mainly exist in large businesses where communication between management and employees is more remote. The trade union's main role is to negotiate with management, on behalf of employees, to improve working conditions and wages.

Key Terms

Dismissal The ending, by an employer, of the contract of employment with an employee because he or she has broken the contract.

External recruitment When an employee is appointed from outside the organisation.

Health and Safety at Work Act (1974) An act that ensures employees have a degree of protection against having an accident or contracting a disease at their place of work.

Induction Training given to a new employee starting a job so that he or she can get used to the place and the people who work there.

Internal recruitment Recruiting the workforce from within the organisation.

Interview The most common method of selection. This is a face-to-face meeting between the candidate and the employer to find out whether the applicant will be suitable for the job, and vice versa.

Job description A detailed written account agreed between employers and employees of the duties and the responsibilities that make up a particular job.

Motivation The reason, or incentive, for doing something. It is especially important when assessing the reasons why people work.

Perk (fringe benefits) Payment in kind over and above the wage or salary, such as extra holiday, staff discount, or a company car.

Person specification A description of the detailed features of the person required to do a job, e.g. experience, qualifications, attitude etc.

Personnel (Human Resources) department The department within a firm that is responsible for the relationship between the employer and employee and for the employee's general welfare.

Recruitment The process of obtaining a supply of new workers to enter an organisation that is usually the responsibility of a human resources department in larger organisations.

Redundancy The situation that results when an employee's contract of employment is ended because that job no longer exists or is no longer needed, i.e. a factory might close down which would make all the workforce redundant.

Trade union An organisation that represents employees at work.

Training The process of improving and extending a person's skills or knowledge.

Unemployment Having no work.

Unfair dismissal The ending of a person's employment by an employer without good reason, for example, a result of discriminating against someone because of their race or sex.

Working conditions A general term used to describe the physical conditions under which a job takes place, e.g. heat, light, noise etc.

ACTIVITY

Try out this role play in pairs. Imagine you and your partner are working in a large supermarket. You are working as a shelf stacker or checkout assistant, and you are also the trade union representative. Your partner represents the management of the supermarket.

There are some issues of concern:

a   mending a broken door that is creating a nasty draught

b   providing a more comfortable chair which does not hurt your back

c   providing a cleaner staff toilet which does not smell.

You and your partner are going to negotiate the above issues. Remember that you are representing the staff in the supermarket. The staff are fed up with the above situations and have approached you to negotiate on their behalf. Your partner has to remember that he or she represents the management. Issues such as cost and staff attitude concern them most.

The Finance function

The Finance Department deals with all the financial matters in the business. The modern finance department has an extensive data processing system backed up by computers.

The main functions of the finance department are:

*   obtaining financial information from different departments
*   recording financial information (this is commonly known as book-keeping)
*   working out payment of staff wages/salaries

*   providing information about the amount of money (capital) needed to run the business efficiently
*   analysing and interpreting financial information
*   providing information about the business's performance to teams and shareholders.

The activities within the finance department include:

*   raising invoices and obtaining payment for goods or services supplied to customers
*   making sure that invoices from suppliers match the goods or services that are supplied to the organisation
*   dealing with payments to suppliers.
*   paying staff
*   dealing with debts
*   analysing the financial performance
*   providing financial information on business performance to managers and shareholders
*   arranging loans and additional finance for the business.

Preparing accounts

One of the main functions of a finance department is to record and keep financial records (accounts) so that the firm can keep track of how much money has come in and how much money has gone out. This allows costs to be measured against revenue (income) so that it is possible to calculate levels of profits or losses made. The Finance Department also has to supply accounts to the Inland Revenue for tax purposes, and keep accurate records of all VAT (Value Added Tax) for Customs and Excise. Another job of the Finance Department is to produce the annual report if the company is a public limited company

(PLC). You will learn about public limited companies in Unit 2 (see page 62).

ACTIVITY

Finish off the following sentences:

1   If a business's revenues are more than its costs it will make a ....
2   If a business's costs are more than its revenue it will make a .... *Loss*
3   A business has to pay .... to the Inland Revenue if it makes ....

Management accounting

One of the main functions of the Finance Department is not only to obtain financial information, but also to analyse this information. This analysis is important because it helps managers to make the right decisions about the running of the business and find out how well the business is doing. and helps them to make decisions about the business. For example, the Finance Department keeps accurate records of all payments so it will be able to help the marketing department decide on prices.

Ismat Niaz, Finance Manager

Ismat has been working at Light Delight Ltd for three years. When she left school she got a job as a trainee accountant in a property development company. After she qualified, she worked in various accountancy firms and later had a few years out of employment when her children were young. She joined Light Delight as Assistant Finance Manager and was promoted to Finance Manager 18 months ago.

Ismat's main responsibilities are:

• To decide on the business credit policy.

• To ensure the effectiveness of the payroll system.

• To make sure that outstanding bills are paid and money has been collected.

• To make sure that the business's financial books are balanced and kept in order.

• To decide on the best method of obtaining finance for the business.

• To ensure that the company's activities are profitable.

Ismat recently expressed concern that too many customers were allowed too high a level of credit.

She meets regularly with the credit controller to discuss the existing credit policy.

Ismat also looks after the book-keeping, and is responsible for staff wages. She has to check the time sheets for staff, to make out wages and has to make the deductions and complete the return for tax and insurance. A daybook is kept which returns the financial transactions which have taken place, and Ismat checks that there is a correct balance. A record also has to be kept for the VAT.

What she/he does

The Finance Department will be able to help managers decide which are the profitable lines of the business (and which might be expanded) and which might be making a loss (so management can improve matters). Sometimes a business may have a 'cash flow' problem. (The business needs to buy a lot of raw materials or goods for resale – and pay for these – before it receives money from its customers.) The Finance Department will know if there is likely to be a problem and will arrange a loan with the bank.

Obtaining capital and resources

One of the aims of many organisations is to grow. In order to grow the business will need money to invest in new equipment, more raw materials, developing new products, larger buildings. All this costs money (and it could be several years before the business starts to make extra profits). Therefore the business will need to borrow money to expand. Limited companies (see page 61) may sell more shares. All businesses will go to banks for loans. It is the Finance Department that arranges the sale of more shares or makes arrangements with the bank.

Paying wages and salaries

The Finance Department is responsible for the payment of wages and salaries. If employees are paid weekly, this is normally called a wage and if employees are paid monthly, this is normally called a salary. Wages and salaries are the returns (payment) for people who work (labour). Whether payment is made by cash, cheque or credit transfer to the bank account, the employee receives a pay advice. This is usually a slip of paper that is filled in by the wages section in the Finance Department and often done by computer. Employees can see how much their gross pay is and what deductions there are.

There are two different types of deductions:

1 compulsory deductions such as income tax and National Insurance

2 voluntary deductions such as union membership fees, contributions to company social club, private pension schemes, private medical schemes (e.g. BUPA) payments.

What employees actually receive is called net pay. This is the amount of money left after all deductions have been made.

Key Terms

Accounts The financial records of a business that are used by managers, owners, employees, creditors and others to show how well the business is doing.

Finance department Deals with all the financial matters in the business.

Gross pay Is the total amount earned by the employee before any deductions have been made.

Income tax Money deducted from each wage/salary payment through the PAYE (Pay As You Earn) system.

National Insurance Is a weekly or monthly contribution to the state welfare scheme (e.g. health services) taken from each payment of wages/salaries. Both employers and employees make a contribution to this scheme.

Net pay The amount of money an employee receives after deductions have been made for income tax, national insurance and any voluntary contribution.

Pay The reward for labour providing its service, usually comprising either a weekly wage or a monthly salary.

Payment system A method of organising the payment of employees, i.e. time rate, piece rate and bonus.

Salary A type of payment to an employee where a certain sum is negotiated on an annual basis and is paid monthly. Salaries are common for payment of workers in professional, managerial and scientific employment.

Tax The compulsory contribution of money to the government. It is a major source of income to the government.

Wage The basic reward paid for the provision of labour as a factor of production. A wage is usually paid on an hourly or weekly basis.

The Administration function

This function deals with the internal housekeeping of the organisation. Administration, secretarial and clerical costs can account for a high percentage of business costs, so it is essential that this part of an organisation is run efficiently.

The main role of the administration function is to provide office services for all other departments in the business, for example:

- collecting and distributing mail
- dealing with and responding to enquiries
- organising meetings
- filing and keeping records
- cleaning and maintaining the workplace
- security.

Other functions include:

- data and word processing
- photocopying
- dealing with e-mails
- switchboard and reception.

Collecting and distributing mail

The administration department deals with the collection and the distribution of incoming mail.

Large organisations will have a specialised mail room that receives all the incoming mail. Small organisations will receive their mail from the postman and it may be opened by the owner or the manager or his or her secretary.

Mail must be opened quickly, sorted accurately and distributed promptly, so that managers and staff can organise their work priorities for the day, know what needs "chasing up" and act on the most up-to-date information available.

Sorting the mail

When mail has been sorted the office clerk must read what is written on the envelope and react accordingly.

Marked	Action
Mail marked urgent	Open immediately
Mail marked personal or private and confidential	Never open
Recorded Delivery	Sign for the delivery and keep record in the Mail Register
Mail wrongly delivered	Re-post unopened
1st and 2nd class mail	Open 1st class first: it is more likely to have urgent information

ACTIVITY: SORTING MAIL

Mail is often placed in mail baskets for distribution or collection. Rearrange the following mail in the right order by starting with the most important one and ending with the least important.

Circulars and magazines, 1st class mail, urgent letters, 2nd class mail, private and confidential or personal letters, wrongly delivered letters.

Dealing with and responding to enquiries

A business's success is determined, to a great extent, by the way it deals with stakeholders' enquiries and how the business communicates generally with its stakeholders. Stakeholders are people who have an interest in a business's activities, and they include customers, suppliers, employees, management and shareholders. The administration department in a business is often the first point of contact when stakeholders telephone. They may be able to deal with stakeholders' enquiries, including customer enquiries, themselves or they will direct the caller to the person or department in the organisation who can deal with the query. In this way, the administration department fulfils an important customer service function. A business will be able to deal with those people's enquiries by establishing an effective communication system. For example, a large proportion of business today is conducted on the telephone. Unfortunately, receiving and making telephone calls is probably one of the most dreaded jobs for the inexperienced office worker. Fears, for example might include giving the wrong information or getting a message muddled.

ACTIVITY

1 What other fears might face a telephonist who deals with customer or supplier enquiries?
2 Make a list of the personal skills that are needed by an office worker or an employee dealing with enquiries. (Activity contd. over page.)

Renata Ottolini, Office Manager

Renata was appointed to work as Assistant Administration Manager at Light Delight Ice Cream Ltd.

"Some people don't appreciate how the administration function is a very important function in the business – it co-ordinates the functions of the other department", Renata says.

She explains how her job is very demanding. For example she has to monitor the collection and distribution of mail each day, the setting up of computers for staff use, electronic mail, cleaning and maintenance etc.

Renata has an administration assistant, Emma Baker, who has been working at Light Delight for 2 years.

Emma Jebson, Administration Assistant

Emma's main job roles are:

- **To ensure** that all mail and correspondence is opened daily.
- **To file** and keep records.
- **To ensure** that all the mail marked urgent or private or confidential or personal is sorted out as soon as possible and distributed to staff.
- **To ensure** that the mail is delivered to the right people.
- **To ensure** that the place is clean and well maintained.

She is also required to carry out some routine tasks, e.g. photocopying, filing, answering telephone calls and ordering stationery.

Activity contd.

3 Compare the above list with your partner's list and write all the personal skills that you have thought of in a separate list.
4 Discuss your and your partner's list with other members of the group.
5 Imagine you are an angry customer of one of the banks who rang to complain about a mistake in his/her bank statement. You play the role of the customer and your partner the role of the telephonist who deals with enquiry.

Organising meetings

When organising meetings, always remember to:

- identify the purpose of the meeting
- make the necessary arrangements, e.g. when and where
- contact, in good time, all people who should attend the meeting
- make the necessary arrangements for refreshments

- make the arrangements for car park facilities
- make the arrangements for any necessary equipment, e.g. overhead projectors.

The agenda for the meeting is the list of items to be dealt with, for example:

- apologies for absence
- minutes of last meeting
- reports
- any other business (AOB)
- date for next meeting.

Writing the minutes

Sometimes the manager asks one of the administrative clerks to attend the meeting to take minutes (the record of what was said). These are typed up afterwards and circulated to all the people who attended.

Filing and keeping records

In any business there is a need to file and keep records about suppliers, customers and other stakeholders. An effective filing system helps the business to operate efficiently for the following reasons:

- up-to-date information can be found immediately
- queries can be answered immediately
- time and effort can be saved in finding the relevant and required information.

What is a good filing system?

A filing system must be easy to understand and use for everyone requiring access to it. Where a number of departments require access to the same information, a centralised filing system is often set up for the whole company. However, most departments also

---

Agenda for Monthly Marketing meeting, Thursday 20th July 2000

1 Apologies for absence

2 Minutes of last meeting

3 Reports

4 AOB

5 Date of next meeting

Emma Jebson
Admin Assistant

Agenda

Minutes for Monthly Marketing meeting, Thursday 20th July 2000

Present:
Gayle Wilkinson, Managing Director
Mike Johnson, Marketing Manager
Louise Carr, Customer Services Manager

Emma Jebson (Admin Assistant)

1 **Apologies**
Apologies were received from Liz Dyson, Production manager, who was on holiday.

2 **Minutes of last meeting**
The minutes of the previous meeting were read and signed as being a true record.

3 **Reports**
Mike Johnson reported that the promotional leaflets which had been sent out to supermarkets with details of Light Delight's new summer ice cream flavors had gone down well. Lots of orders had been received for these new products.

4 **AOB**
Louise Carr, Customer Service Manager, reported that there had been a few complaints about some of the ice cream cartons being sticky on the outside. The production department were already aware of the problem, however, and hoped the problem would be sorted out by the end of the week.

5 The date of the next meeting was set for Thursday 24th August.

Signed

Minutes

file relevant information within their own sections. To make these systems easy to understand and use, it is helpful to display a set of instructions on the current filing system that everybody in the administration department can follow.

Filing confidential information

A locked drawer with limited access to keys should be provided in which to file all confidential documents. Confidential documents that are not required any more should be destroyed.

Most businesses use computers to record and keep information. Information is kept in database programs. The names of files are kept in a directory that contains information on the size of every file and dates when they were created. Confidential files can be password protected.

Cleaning and maintaining the workplace

According to the Health and Safety at Work Act (1974), all employers and employees are responsible for the health and safety of the workplace. Employers must make sure that the place is clean and well maintained for employees to work effectively. Hazardous situations usually result from poor maintenance and a dirty or unclean workplace. For example, wet floors or poorly lit areas can cause accidents such as falls or slips. Faulty machines can cause electric shocks and accidents.

The administration staff in large businesses are involved in organising cleaning and keeping the workplace tidy and well maintained. They must be aware of what makes for organising a safe workplace.

Security

Some of the administration staff in large organisations work in a security department. Their job is to make sure the workplace is secure and no strangers are on the premises of whom they are not aware. They check buildings after staff leave and make sure all doors are locked and security cameras are in operation.

They also deal with visitors who come to visit the business. Many large businesses have a gatehouse where security staff check visitors as they enter the premises and issue a special visitor's badge. Visitors' badges may be colour-coded to show which areas the visitor has access to and which he or she has not. The visitor will also be asked to "sign in" using the Visitor's Book. He or she will write down his or her name, the organisation he or she belongs to, the date, and his or her car registration number. The gatehouse will also check out visitors as they leave and take back their badges.

Reception

Some of the administration staff in medium to large businesses work on the reception. Most large offices employ receptionists to act as the first point of contact when someone enters the building. Because the people who work on reception are the first people you will meet when you go into a business, it is very important that they are polite, well presented and helpful. If they give a good impression, this reflects on the business. A receptionist is very often also the first person you will speak to if you telephone the company, and it is his or her job to deal with your enquiry or put you through to another person in the business who can help you. In this way, receptionists provide an important customer service function. Receptionists therefore need to have a good understanding of the business, the people who work for it and its customers.

ACTIVITY

1 Find out from the reception or office staff in your school or college what security procedure the school or college follows when someone visits.

2 Find out why visitors are asked to write down their car registration number in the Visitor's Book.

The Production function

Production is at the heart of any organisation. In a manufacturing company it turns raw materials (sheet metal, cocoa beans) into finished products (washing machines, bars of chocolate). The type of production will depend on the end product – the production or building of an ocean liner will be very different from the production of chocolate mini-eggs.

In the service sector, production is the process by which a service is provided to a customer.

Liz Dyson, Production Manager

Liz's role at Light Delight Ltd started even before the company was set up. She set up the business and was very keen that it should succeed.

Liz's main responsibilities are:

- **To plan** the best way to make ice-cream.
- **To introduce** new ideas to improve the product.
- **To purchase** the necessary raw materials at the lowest price and highest quality.
- **To make sure** that the quality of ice-cream is of the highest standard.
- **To ensure** that the machines are in good working order.
- **To decide** on the best and safest method of production.
- **To plan** with the Managing Director when equipment should be replaced.
- **To check** regularly that the production team is adequately trained, especially when new production processes are introduced.

- **To check** that her team is working to Health and Safety regulations and ensure her team is supervised at all times.
- **To ensure** that all equipment and tools are well looked after and stored away safely.

Every day Liz checks that everyone in her team has arrived on time. She checks the weekly rota of duties to see that everything is covered. She has to notify the human resources/personnel department of the absence of any member of the team.

At midnight she makes a tour of the production department to check that everything is operating smoothly.

During lunch time she has an informal discussion with her Production Assistant Managers to make sure that everything is in order.

Liz is required to present a progress report at the weekly meeting with the Managing Director.

She is also required to prepare a more detailed report for the monthly Board of Director's meeting.

(Often in the service sector it is called "Operations".) For example, a company which sells insurance will have different types of policy, and a theme park will develop new attractions and rides.

Planning is a very important part of Production:

- What raw materials will be needed? How many?

CASE STUDY – Production at Light Delight Ltd

Mr Grey has just bought a "family block" of ice cream. As he leaves the local shop his daughter asks him where the ice cream comes from. He answered 'cows'. Darren the shop keeper knows that before he sells the ice cream he has to order it from the factory. The factory is called Light Delight Ice Cream. Irene works at the factory in the administration department. She takes orders over the phone or by letters or e-mails and passes them to Emma who types them into the firm's computer. Carol also makes out the bill/invoice for Darren's shop.

In order to make the ice cream Asha the Production Assistant Manager for Purchasing has to order the raw materials, such as milk powder, sugar or fruit. She uses the computer to check what raw materials are not available in stock and therefore need to be ordered (stock control), and how much ice cream needs to be made that day.

There was a time when it took three or more people to mix and freeze the ice cream. These days, with the development in new technology, it can be done with computer-controlled machines. The frozen ice cream is forced along pipes (at the beginning of the production lineunder high pressure until it comes out of a tap at the other end of the production line where Liz sits, waiting to collect the ice cream in plastic containers. Then she passes these to Ahmed who seals them with lids so that

Gemma can take them into a cold store to be frozen solid. Then Mary and Carl will transfer them on to shelves in the refrigerated warehouse.

Terry and David, the warehouse foremen, control the despatch of stock. To help the lorry drivers they have to arrange all the boxes of ice cream in the correct order for loading and delivery. They also help the driver to load up the refrigerated lorries.

Only then can the ice cream be delivered to shops or supermarkets.

Read the above case study carefully and use examples to answer the following questions:

1 What are the natural resources, e.g. raw materials, that are needed to make ice cream?
2 What are the human resources that are needed to make ice cream?
3 What are the man-made resources, e.g. machinery and equipment, needed to make ice cream?
4 Explain the effect of the use of computers on the production process in the Light Delight ice cream factory.
5 When do you think the role of the purchase function takes place in the above factory?
6 Visit your local supermarket and choose an ice cream container. Find out the ingredients which are used to produce it

- What will need to be stored?
- What machines will be needed?
- Who will operate the machines?
- Do these people need to be hired? Will they need training?
- How long will it take to produce the item?
- Will it need to be stored?

For service industries similar planning must take place. In eductaion, the government needs to plan how many school places to provide, what subjects will be taught, the number of teachers who need to be trained, the computers and books that need to be bought – all within a budget.

Key Terms

Administration department The department which deals with all the administration activities in a business, for example, filing records and organising meetings.

Agenda A list of items to be discussed in a meeting, e.g., plans for a new factory, employing more people, reporting accidents, etc.

Consumer A person who buys goods and services for his or her own use or consumption.

Employees People who are employed by the owners or managers of a business. They get paid a wage or salary for working in the business.

Goods A general term used to represent the wide variety of items that are produced as a result of economic activity.

Human resources People (labour) that work in the business, e.g. managers, supervisors, cashiers, etc.

Natural resources Raw materials which come from the land and are used to make final products, e.g., wool is used to make jumpers and coats, and wheat grain is used to make flour and bread.

Production The process by which an organisation transforms raw materials, using financial and human resources into an end product that is consumed by someone else, for example, bread.

Purchasing An important function in organisations dealing with the purchase of the materials necessary to allow the goods or services of that organisation to be produced.

Service sector Sometimes called the tertiary sector, this includes all services such as banking, insurance, education, policing etc.

Stakeholders Anyone who has an interest in a business's activities and who can therefore influence business decisions. Stakeholders include a business's customers, suppliers, employees, management and shareholders.

Stock control The process of trying to establish the best level of stocks to hold.

The Marketing and Sales function

Marketing is responsible for finding out and satisfying customer needs and wants. Good marketing can be the key to the success of a business

Customers will buy a product only if it will help them:

- to do something that they cannot do now
- to do something better than they can do it now
- to do something more quickly than they can do it now
- to do something more easily than they can do it now
- to do something more cost effectively (more cheaply) than they can do it now
- to get more satisfaction than they are getting now
- to get something different from what they are getting now.

However, a company or a business will make a profit only if customers buy their good or service at a price that will give them a profit after all production costs have been taken into consideration.

Mike Johnson, Marketing Manager at Light Delight

Mike was appointed as Marketing Manager at Light Delight six years ago. He had previously been working as a sales representative for a large chilled foods manufacturer.

However, when Mike and his wife were divorced and he had to look after their children by himself, he wanted a job which would not involve travelling around the country, so he could be at home when he needed to be. Mike has two assistant managers, Jenny and Raheem, who work under his supervision and are responsible to him.

Mike's main responsibilities are:

- **To formulate**, recommend and implement the company's marketing strategy.

- **To decide** on the best pricing strategy to increase sales and attract more customers.

- **To monitor and implement** the development of a new product.

- **To monitor and analyse** sales figures with his team.

- **To decide** on the best promotion method to promote the ice-cream.

His responsibilities also include doing everything he can to ensure that the company retains 'delighted customers with a delightful ice-cream'.

Mike works very closely with his sales team and encourages their sales efforts. His experience in sales make him good at motivating the sales staff. He meets every week with his Assistant Manager for Sales to make sure that sale targets are met and customers needs and wants are met.

How does marketing do this?

By researching about the market and customers:

1 **Product:** Do customers even know they want this product yet? Will they want an expensive top-of-the-range version or a cheap and cheerful version? Will they want exotic packaging or a plain bag?

2 **Price:** the price must be one that customers see as good value and one that provides good profit for the business. The price should also reflect the image of the product.

3 **Place:** how and where a business makes the product and makes it available to customers. It should make it easy for customers to buy and obtain the product. For example, if you were selling a new sports drink would you make it available in sports centres or supermarkets? When do customers want to buy sports drinks?

4 **Promotion:** only when a business has got the product, price and place right should they promote the product and persuade customers to buy it.

ACTIVITY

Complete the following statement.

The main function of the marketing department in an organisation is to make sure that the right .... is produced at the right .... in the right .... using the right ....

BECKHAM

Market research

Business organisations need to have information that will enable them to make decisions about:

- what products to produce
- whom to produce the products for
- when to produce the products
- how many products to produce
- how to produce the products
- how to make the products look attractive.

Market research is a good way of obtaining information about potential and existing customers' needs and wants. In this section you are going to learn about:

- the meaning of market research
- the stages of market research
- the methods of market research.

What is the meaning of "market research"?

A market researcher carrying out a survey

Market research is finding out information about customer needs and wants, before and after the development of new products, to make sure that these needs and wants are met and customers are satisfied.

What stages are involved in market research?

1 **Asking the right questions:** Put simply, a business must ask the right questions to get useful answers that can help them during product development.

2 **Finding out who and where the customers are:** Businesses must clearly identify the potential customers at whom the product will be targeted. For example, if a business decides to develop a new and expensive perfume, it must first identify the customers at whom the product will be aimed.

In this case, the target market would be women who enjoy trying new fragrances and have enough money to be able to afford the perfume.

The methods of market research

Once a business decides who its target customers are, the next stage of the market research is to choose the methods of research to ascertain how to reach the target market.

Two methods are usually adopted:

1 **Field research:** This method of research is used to collect information or data directly from the market. This data is called **primary data.**

   Primary data is information not already in published form and which must, therefore, be obtained by the business. Examples of field research methods are questionnaires, interviews, observing customers on the shop floor, tests in the market before the launch of a new product, and analysing sales records.

2 **Desk research:** This method of research is used to collect **secondary data.**

   Secondary data is information collected for specific purposes such as government statistics, trade publications, and published academic research. You do not need to go out into the field to collect it. It has already been collected for other purposes and is recorded.

ACTIVITY: THE ADVANTAGES AND DISADVANTAGES OF RESEARCH METHODS

Each research method has advantages and disadvantages. Draw a table with three headings – **Research method, Advantages, Disadvantages.** Write the heading **Advantages** in black and the heading **Disadvantages** in red. Find out the advantages and disadvantages of the following research methods:

- questionnaires
- interviews
- observing customers' attitudes and behaviour on the shop floor
- testing the market before the launch of a new product
- analysing sales records.

Consider the following points:
- time required to collect the information
- effort required to collect the information
- cost of collecting the information
- accuracy of the information collected
- ease of access
- number of people who are approached.

1 Fill in the table using the above criteria.
2 From the information in the table, write down the advantages and disadvantages of field research and desk research.

ACTIVITY: MARKET RESEARCH

In this activity you are going to learn how to carry out market research.

The list below is for the top ten cereals from the British Market Research Bureau's 1991 Target Group Index (the survey was carried out among 25,600 adults between April 1990 and March 1991). It is a detailed study of regular purchases, shopping habits and lifestyle. It is not a market research study.

Type of cereal	Percentage of buyers
Kellogg's Corn Flakes	43.1%
Weetabix	41.8%
Kellogg's Rice Krispies	28.5%
Kellogg's Frosties	20.3%
Shredded Wheat	17.0%
Kellogg's Crunchy Nut Flakes	16.1%
Kellogg's Bran Flakes	15.4%
Kellogg's All-Bran	12.0%
Sugar Puffs	11.8%
Alpen	10.6%

1 From this list find out:
   a the number of cereal products which are made by Kellogg's
   b the number of cereal products which are supermarket own brands
   c the number of cereal products which are sugar-coated
   d which cereal products are associated with healthier eating

   e the brand of cereal that is most popular
   f the brand of cereal that is least popular.
2 Using your IT skills, present the above table as a bar chart.
3 Ask all members of the group which cereals they eat for breakfast. Make a list of the group's top ten breakfast cereals.
4 Present the findings of the group survey in a similar table to the one above.
5 Using your IT skills, present the group survey table as bar charts.
6 Compare the students' top ten with the list above for the top ten cereals:
   a Are there any products which are on the group's list?
   b Which products are not in the national top ten?
   c Is it possible to draw any conclusion?

Promotion

Promotion means informing the customers about the product and persuading them to buy it. All businesses are regularly involved in promotional activities to make sure that customers do not forget their products (the goods they produce or the services they supply).

In general terms, there are three main aims of promotion:

1 to inform customers about a new product
2 to persuade customers to buy the product
3 to promote the product.

The aim and type of promotion will affect the range and style of the promotional materials. As an example, a university may produce quite formal brochures and booklets with photographs of the campus, facilities and students' accommodation. A promotional leaflet from McDonald's is likely to be far more informal with a different style of wording and less formal illustrations.

You can find us at 43 The High Street
(next to the ABC Cinema)

A promotional flyer for a new sandwich shop

ACTIVITY

In your groups, list five different methods which businesses use to persuade customers to buy their products.

Each member of the group has to think of a recent example of a business that tries to persuade customers to buy its products.

Why use promotional materials?
All businesses use promotional materials to achieve the following objectives:

1   To create demand by:

- persuading customers that they will benefit from buying the product or service
- giving information about new or improved products or services
- giving information about special offers
- keeping the name of the business and/or the product at the forefront of the customer's mind.

2   To increase demand by:

- persuading existing customers to buy more of the product
- attracting more potential customers to the product.

3   To create sales by:

- informing people about where and how they can obtain the product or service
- building up customer loyalty to a brand or business
- persuading consumers that this particular product or service is better than those offered by competitors
- creating consumer awareness of a range of products.

ACTIVITY

Discuss in your groups how your local supermarket tries to build customer loyalty.

Ask yourselves the following questions:

a Does it have a petrol station?
b Does it offer a loyalty card for shoppers?
c Is there any other service which you can obtain from your local supermarket, for example, restaurant, or chemist?

4   To influence customer perceptions by:

- improving general awareness of the business and its policies
- creating a favourable image in the mind of the public.

The image created may simply be to convince consumers that the business has good customer relations, is environmentally friendly and provides quality products. The hope is that the public will think highly of this company and therefore buy its goods.

A business will achieve the objectives of creating demand and increasing sales only if the promotional materials themselves:

a   attract the attention of consumers

b   gain their interest by, for example, including special offers or eye-catching pictures

c   create a desire to own the product or to buy the service

d   explain to the consumers how they can take action, for example, where goods are on sale, what they must do next.

Forms of promotion

Promotion takes two forms:

1   advertising
2   sales promotion.

1   Advertising

Advertising is the presenting of a product to the public to encourage sales – it can have spectacular results.

For example, in 1996, jeans manufacturers such as Levi's suddenly switched to using female models in their television adverts. Sales of jeans shot through the roof.

ACTIVITY

Look through three or four magazines and newspapers. Select ten advertisements that attract your attention and make you interested.

Analyse what it was that caught your eye and made you interested. What features of the advertisement do you think have been deliberately included to create desire.

Look around the area where you live and find examples of three posters that attract your attention. Look for those with a strong, clever, interesting, eye-catching or witty headline, message or design. Describe the position of each of these posters, i.e. near a supermarket, a bank or an airport. Give examples of the types of goods advertised.

Media is the method used to communicate with the public. Types of advertising media include newspapers, television, commercial radio, direct mail, cinema and posters.

2   Sales promotion

Sales promotion is often thought of as being the same as advertising. However, although the objectives of promotion and advertising are the same (to persuade the consumer to buy), there are differences in the way they are practised. Sales promotion often takes the form of an incentive, e.g. a free sample or a special offer.

There are many methods of sales promotion such as:

Logos These are symbols used by companies so that its adverts and products are instantly recognisable. Both logos and trademarks are protected by law once they have been registered by a company. No one else can use or reproduce them without the company's permission.

Slogans These are often employed because they are memorable. "Put a tiger in your tank" was a famous Esso slogan for many years. The benefit of a short, punchy slogan is that it is easily remembered and becomes associated with the product (or company).

Another way of making adverts memorable is to make them **humorous**. Two of the most famous and successful campaigns have been the PG Tips and Heineken adverts.

ACTIVITIES

1 Find out the logo for each of the following:
   a Virgin Trains
   b Barclays Bank
   c Toyota Cars
   d British Telecom
   e Kentucky Fried Chicken.
2 Collect a minimum of six adverts from newspapers or magazines that you think use either a good slogan, humour or some other device that attracts you.
3 Which companies use the following slogans?
   "Everything we do is driven by you."
   "It's the real thing."
   "Helps you work, rest and play."
   "The ultimate driving machine."

For each one, note down the features you like.

Branding

A company uses packaging and labels or trademarks to separate its product from those of its rivals. This is called "branding" and brand names are a common form of promotion. Branding does not stop with

just the name – it translates through to packaging design and colour.

ACTIVITY

1 Find a picture of a bar of chocolate and explain why it is attractive.
2 Visit a local supermarket and select three products where colour has been used effectively for the packaging or container.
3 Write a summary of each one. State the product and its purpose. Why do you think the colours used were chosen?

Personal appearances
Celebrities often appear on "television programmes" (e.g. 'TFI Friday') to promote a new product. Authors and sports people sometimes make personal appearances at bookshops to sign copies of their novels to promote sales.

Exhibitions and demonstrations
Many products are displayed at exhibitions open to the general public. A product may sometimes be tested by the public in a supermarket. In large department stores, aftershave and perfumes are available for testing.

Sampling
One method of promoting a new product is to provide free samples of it to households. The company hopes that once consumers have tried a small sachet sample of the product, they will go and buy the larger size bottle or packet at the shop.

Special offers
Some businesses give their customers special offers to promote and increase sales, i.e. buy one get one free, or selling a bigger pack of a product at the same price as the smaller one.

ACTIVITY

Visit one or two of the big retailers in your local area. Find out examples of special offers on some products (goods or services).

Pricing promotions
The idea behind a pricing promotion is to try to persuade consumers that they are getting value for money. A seasonal sale, to clear out stock from the previous season to make room for the new season's collection, is an example of a pricing promotion, e.g. summer sale or Christmas sale.

Direct mail
The use of computers to maintain consumer records has enabled more and more companies to use mailing methods to promote their products.

GROUP ACTIVITY

In your groups, think of three businesses that sell their products by direct mail. What do you think are the advantages of this method?

Sponsorship
This is frequently done to promote the name of the company rather than a particular product. For example, Sainsbury's and Tesco sponsor Art School kits, events and computer equipment.

GROUP ACTIVITY

In your group, think of an event either in your school or college or in your local area that was sponsored by big business, for example, collecting coupons from large supermarkets for school computers. Think about the benefits of this sponsorships for both businesses and your local community.

The sales function

The sales function is the responsibility of the sales department in a large organisation or business. However, in small businesses, the sales function is usually a part of the marketing function.

The main responsibilities of the sales department are to identify potential customers and encourage them to buy, and to deal directly with customers and provide

(contd. on page 39)

Key Terms

Advertising The process of informing a customer about a product or service, and persuading that customer to buy it.

Advertising media The channels through which businesses and other organisations communicate with their customers, for example, newspapers, TV, billboards etc.

Brand A trade name or trademark created for a product in order to persuade the customer that this product is different from that of competitors, e.g. Coca-Cola.

Competition The idea that in a market one producer should always be rivalled by another producer to ensure that prices are kept low and the customer is not exploited.

Consumer A person who buys goods and services for his or her own use or consumption.

Customer A person who buys a product either for his or her own use or for someone else. For example, if your friend buys you a CD for your birthday, he is the customer and you are the consumer. All businesses work very hard to please customers and satisfy their needs.

Demand The desire or need of a consumer backed up by the ability to pay over a period of time.

Desk research It is a research method to collect secondary data, e.g. company's old records.

Field research It is a research method to collect primary data, e.g. interviews and questionnaires

Logo A symbol or picture, often based on a brand name or trademark, which is used by a company to help consumers identify and remember their products.

Marketing Finding out about customer demand, and the satisfaction of that demand by the development, distribution and exchange of goods and services.

Market research The finding out of information about customers' needs and wants to help with the making of marketing decisions.

Price The market value of goods and services that are bought by consumers and firms.

Primary data Information not already in published material and which must, therefore, be obtained by the researcher. Primary data is obtained from the field research.

Promotion The various ways by which an organisation attempts to persuade consumers to purchase its product, e.g. advertising and special offers. It is one of the four elements of the marketing mix.

Secondary data Information collected for a specific purpose such as government statistics, trade publications and published academic research. You do not need to go out into the field to collect it, e.g. data from books or magazines.

Survey A piece of research carried out to establish the opinions and attitudes of individuals to an existing or new product.

Trademark A particular logo that a business uses to distinguish its product from another one. Examples are Nike and Coca-Cola.

customer support. In this way, they are fulfilling an important customer service function.

The Customer Service function

All of the functional areas work towards providing the customer service function. It is essential that a business looks after its customers if it wants to remain in business. Although all of the functional areas are concerned with customer service, most companies also have a special department which looks after the customers after they have bought something from the company. The customer services department provides an after sales service and deals with customer enquiries. Information about the customer service function and customer services department can be found in chapter 3.

How departments within an organisation work together

All the functions within a company are interdependent. For example, it is pointless having a very efficient finance/accounting function if the firm's marketing function is extremely inefficient. Similarly, a business may have an excellent marketing department but sell few products because of a low standard of quality.

To be successful, a business also needs a motivated workforce that is willing to work hard. Therefore, it is very important that the human resources department liaises with other departments to ensure that employees are happy and motivated.

ACTIVITY: WHICH DIRECTOR TO LIAISE WITH

In this activity you are going to learn how different functional directors need to liaise with other functional directors.

Fill in the gaps in the following sentences by using one of the following directors:

Marketing; Sales; Human Resources; Production; Finance; Administration.

1   The Sales Director works closely with the .... Director to ensure that the sales plan is implemented and monitored.

2   The Marketing Director liaises with the .... Director to identify the skills and experience of his team members.

3   The Marketing Director liaises with the .... Director to manage and check quality, at the design and development stage and regularly throughout production.

4   The Production Director should liaise with the ...., and .... Directors to determine a selling price for a new product.

5   The Human Resources Director liaises with the ...., ..., ..., and .... Directors to ensure that all company members are motivated and adequately trained for the job they are expected to do.

6   The Production Director liaises with the .... and .... Directors on working out the cost and the design of the product.

7   The Production Director liaises with the .... to ensure that the production team complies with the health and safety regulations.

8   The .... department works closely with the production, finance, marketing, sales and human resources departments to ensure the accessibility of communication and the flow of information between them.

ACTIVITIES: FUNCTIONS IN A BUSINESS

The aims of this activity are:

To understand more about the functions within a business.

To apply and relate these functions to different departments in the business.

To understand how these functions are linked and related to the stakeholders (people who influence business decisions).

I Work out which department (Production, Marketing, Finance, Human resources, Customer Service, Administration) would carry out the following functions.

  a Training of human resources
  b Advertising
  c Marketing
  d Recruitment
  e Holidays
  f Job advertisements
  g Sending application forms
  h Writing job specifications
  i Purchasing raw materials
  j The delivery of goods to customers in time
  k Typing pool and data processing
  l Quality control
  m Dealing with faulty goods
  n Payment of wages
  o Organising the flow of money in and out of the business
  p Make customers aware of new products
  q Dealing with customers' complaints

2 You have learned before that there are different groups of people (stakeholders) who influence business decisions, e.g. customers, shareholders, employees and trade unions.

Revise what you have learnt in Chapter 2 and try to answer the following questions:

  a Which department deals directly with customers?
  b Which department/departments deals indirectly with customers?
  c Which department deals with suppliers of raw materials?
  d Which department deals directly with employees in the business?
  e Which department/departments might deal directly with the local community?
  f Which department might deal with the financial affairs of the shareholders?

3 Which department/departments will be interested in recording and keeping the following information?

  a Information about the employee pay roll.
  b Information about a new advertising campaign.
  c Information about a new design for a product.
  d Information about how employees are paid.
  e Information about a new service to customers.
  f Information about the cost of new machinery.

4 "Effective administration function results in a good customer service."

In your groups discuss the above statement. Explain how an effective process of keeping and recording customer information could improve customer service.

Chapter 3 Customer service

Customer service means that the company is concerned with keeping the customer happy and satisfied. It is the job of all of the functional areas (departments) described in chapter 2 to make sure the company's customers are satisfied. For example, the Production Department must produce goods which are not faulty, and the Marketing Department needs to give customers the correct information. If the Marketing Department put the wrong prices in a catalogue, for instance, customers would get upset. All of the functional areas in a business work together to provide good customer service, because without customers there would not be a business. Most companies also have a department dedicated especially to customer service, which provides an after-sales service once a customer has bought a product from the company. The term customer service is used here to describe the way in which all functions of a business work together to ensure good customer service. Once the company has sold a product to the customer, the customer services department must see that the consumer is content with the product.

A dissatisfied customer may be a future sale lost and bad publicity.

A customer service department should be aware that all customers have the following rights:

- to find out information about the product
- to choose a product
- to buy a product
- to get value for money.
- to be satisfied and well looked after once the product has been purchased.

What does good quality customer service mean?

You will usually be able to buy what you want in more than one shop, but the range of goods, and the help you can expect from the staff can make one shop much more attractive to you than the other. Retailers attract regular customers by offering a good service. This includes:

- a choice of goods
- quality
- competitive prices
- reliable guarantees and after-sales service
- helpful, polite and knowledgeable staff
- pleasant surroundings.

ACTIVITY

1 Think back to a time when you feel you received excellent customer service – it may have been in a shop, restaurant or library. Describe it briefly.
2 Think of the characteristics of the person who provided you with excellent service. Describe this person.

Louise Carr, Customer Service Manager, Light Delight

I joined the company as Customer Service Manager 3 years ago and I am responsible to Mike Johnson, the Marketing Manager. My job after college was as a receptionist in a hospital. I enjoy the contact with people that this gave me, and I decided to get a job in a customer service call centre for a large telecommunications company while studying for an NVQ3 in Customer Service. When I got my NVQ, I decided that I wanted more responsibility, and Customer Service Manager job at Light Selight seemed like an exciting challenge. It certainly has been a challenge so far! I start my day at 8am and I don't finish before 7pm. Although my job is very tiring, I enjoy talking to, and dealing with, customers. The majority of our customers are big food retailers and supermarkets. These days customers have many expectations of a product they buy. They expect value for money, so we must provide them with a good quality product at a reasonable price.

The first thing I do when I get to work is read my e-mails and check whether there are any customer complaints. I ensure that any complaints are dealt with immediately. Most customers' complaints are due to late delivery, especially in summer when the demand for ice-cream is high. When customers order goods and services, it is to satisfy their needs and wants now – we would quickly lose customers if we kept delivering orders late. That is why I have a regular meeting once a week with Liz Dyson, the Production Manager, to ensure that we have enough stock and raw materials to meet supermarket demand. ⟶ wants

I also have regular daily meetings with our sales team to ensure that our customers are satisfied with our product. We know that the ice-cream market is very competitive and if we don't provide good customer service we would lose customers.

In addition, one of my main tasks is to make sure that the ice-cream is available to consumers in shops and make sure that there are enough products reaching the people who want them. Light Delight employs people to organise how often deliveries must be made to the right retailers at the right time.

The most important part of my job is monitor the way customers are treated when they telephone us or visit our factory.

We are responsible for any faults with the ice-cream we sell. The customer automatically has the right to have his or her money back if the goods are faulty. As long as the customer was not responsible for the damage then we must return the customer's money.

Last year, as part of our commitment to customer service, we extend the customers' right to a refund on purchased ice-cream even if the goods are not faulty. For example, if a regular customer, such as a big supermarket like Sava Stores, mistakenly orders the wrong ice-cream flavour, we would give a refund as long as the goods were returned to us on the same day without being damaged or melted. We always manage to sell it to another retailer.

CASE STUDY – Focus Do It All and Customer Service

Focus Do It All (FDIA) is one of the largest DIY retailers in the UK. Do It All belonged to the Boots group until August 1998 when it was sold.

FDIA offers an extensive and exclusive range of tools and materials, complemented by a very high level of customer service from experienced and knowledgeable staff. FDIA has always sought to differentiate itself from its competitors by:

1   offering stylish and innovative products

2   extending an established strength in home decoration

3   increasing the amount of own-label and exclusive lines in stock

4   introducing additional service policies that customers value, for example no-

quibble exchange on returned products even if they have been used.

DIA was highly commended in the 1997 *Daily Telegraph/British Telecom Customer Service Award* and commended in the 1996 Awards in recognition of its commitment to customer service.

Questions

Read the case study carefully and carry out the following tasks:

1   FDIA is highly committed to offering the best customer service. Get evidence from the case study to support this statement.

2   Explain how good quality customer service helps FDIA to compete.

3   Visit the FDIA in your local area. Obtain as much information as you can about the customer service that the store offers.

4   Visit another retailer that offers the same products as FDIA. Try to obtain similar information about its customer service facility.

5   Write a report to compare the customer service in the local FDIA store and the customer service that is offered by the other retailer.

Reasons for good customer service

Businesses are constantly trying to improve customer service for the following reasons:

1   to attract more customers

2   to increase sales

3   to improve a business reputation

4   to be able to compete.

For example, at Halifax PLC, one of the biggest banks in the UK, two of the main factors that contribute to its business success are the Halifax commitment to high standards of service and the expertise of its staff. To maintain these standards and keep staff up to date with new products, the Halifax invests in training.

Example of customer service at Halifax PLC:

- well-trained staff who are always there to help and offer advice
- free mortgage and loans counselling in all Halifax branches
- Halifax Visa Card
- Maxim current account
- Little Extra Club with its colourful money box
- free children's magazines.

Quality customer service means the FIVE C'S:

- Courtesy
- Care
- Communication
- Co-operation
- Compliment.

Effects of bad customer service

Businesses realise that bad customer service means a dissatisfied customer and this could lead to:

- a future sale lost
- bad publicity
- bad business image and reputation.
- inability to cope with the competition.

ACTIVITY: EXAMPLES OF CUSTOMER SERVICE

Salespeople have to deal with a wide range of situations and customers during the course of

a typical day. Classify each of the following situations under the correct area of customer service. In your groups, put forward your ideas and discuss how you would cope with the following situations.

1 A woman insists on trying on an expensive evening dress that is obviously too small for her and there is a definite risk that the dress will split at the seams.
2 A customer returns an expensive squash racket with a broken head. The customer explains that it just snapped when he made contact with the ball. You notice that the top edge of the racket head is well marked. It was purchased about 2 months earlier.
3 You have already shown a customer a large number of suits and a growing number of other people in the shop look as though they need attention. Nobody else is free to help them.
4 You have just started to serve someone when another customer claims that they should have been served first.
5 While his mother is looking at some dresses a little boy eating ice cream is idly brushing his hand along a rack of blouses.
6 You have a group of three young people who hang around inside your newsagent's shop just reading the magazines and occasionally being very familiar with female customers.

Areas covered by customer service

Customer service describes and covers different areas of dealing with customers during and after the purchase of the product. These include:

- the way a customer is treated by sales staff on the telephone, in the shop and at the checkout

- the way queries and complaints are handled
- refunds and replacement of goods
- related services, for example, free delivery, free help-line for customers, extended warranties or guarantees
- providing information about the products, to enable customers to choose the right ones
- assisting customers to use the products
- assisting customers with special needs
- after-sales service. This relates to the help and assistance that is given to customers after the sale has been completed. Customer service does not end with the selling of the product. It is extended after sale to provide the best possible service for the customer.

Many businesses have a dedicated customer service department to assist customers

ACTIVITY

In your group, think of a business that concentrates on giving excellent customer service and often relies on word of mouth rather than advertising to boost the number of its customers.

Customer services and nature of business

The nature and the extent of customer service activities depends on:

1   the nature of business, e.g. retailer manufacturer or service provider

2   the scale of business

3   the type of business ownership, e.g. a sole trader, partnership or Ltd

4   the type of product, e.g. goods or services

5   the use of the product, e.g. for consumer use or for industrial use

6   the competition in the market.

ACTIVITY

Find out the similarities and the differences between customer service activities that should be offered by the following businesses:

1   a big clothes retailer
2   a car manufacturer
3   a food retailer
4   a bank or a building society
5   a water company.

Chapter 4 Business communications

Successful communication between people is a vital activity within an organisation. Good communication not only aids motivation but also improves overall efficiency. The main emphasis of this section will be on communication between the businesses and their stakeholders.

Workplace communication is the passing of information and instructions that help the organisation to operate efficiently.

1 It increases employees' involvement in decision making.

2 It increases employees' satisfaction if they have been involved in decision making.

3 It increases employees' motivation and they will be more committed to their work if the system of communication is efficient.

4 It increases business efficiency, as employees will be more motivated and satisfied.

5 It improves the Industrial relations between management and trade unions.

Types of communication

1 internal communication between colleagues within the same company

2 external communication with outsiders such as customers, shareholders, local community, government, and suppliers (stakeholders).

Methods of communication

There are a number of ways in which a message can be passed from one person to another. Some of these are oral methods and some are written. The best method will depend on the nature of the message.

I Oral communication:

This has the advantage of being quick and allowing immediate response. Problems may arise, however, because there is no written record of the message for referencing at a later date. Also, when the message has to pass down a long chain, there is the possibility of distortion.

Oral methods of communications include:

- meeting
- face-to-face communication
- telephone conversations.

A meeting is a form of oral communication that businesses use

2 Written communication:

This has the advantages that the message is permanent and can be referred to at any time. Information is also likely to be more accurate as greater care will be taken in presenting the information. Written methods are also more appropriate when a business wants a message to be received by a lot of people.

Written methods of communication include:

- letters
- handbooks and manuals produced for reference purpose and dealing with personnel matters or technical details
- employee newsletters to keep workers informed about company activities
- circulars can be used to inform workers or for special events, and to provide important information

- much internal written communication takes place by means of memoranda (memos). A memo is a form of letter which is only used internally and is not usually private (it could be read by anyone in the business)
- the annual report and accounts of a company is a financial report that is made available to shareholders as well as managers. In many cases the report, in the form of a specially produced summary, is made available to employees to keep them informed as to the company's financial position
- e-mails are a new and fast way of communication that can be used as both an internal and external method of communication
- advertisements.

CASE STUDY — Alliance & Leicester

On 21 April 1997, Alliance & Leicester changed from being a building society to being a public limited company, listed on the London Stock Exchange. Alliance & Leicester is a major financial services group dedicated to the provision of a range of personal financial products for customers. Its objective is to provide customers with a comprehensive range of mortgage and other financial and banking services that are high in quality and competitive in price.

Alliance & Leicester has more than five million customers living in the UK. The company uses a wide network of communication whenever and wherever it best suits the needs of customers. For example, Girobank, acquired by Alliance & Leicester in 1990, was the first telephone bank in the UK. More Alliance & Leicester customers are able to use a full 24-hour telephone and postal banking

facility than with any other bank or building society in the UK.

Within Alliance & Leicester, efficient communication provides employees with information that assists their work. Informing employees about developments within the business helps to involve them further and create an understanding of how these developments may affect their daily decisions.

There are two different types of communication at the company:

1 internal communication between management and staff

2 external communication between the company and outsider.

Internal communication at Alliance & Leicester

Communication is not only used by senior managers for giving instructions downwards, but also for passing on business strategy so that more people within the company understand how Alliance & Leicester is working towards its objectives. The communication process also works in the opposite way, from lower to higher levels. Good internal communication enables employees to discuss issues within the workplace.

Various communication methods are used by Alliance & Leicester to motivate employees and improve teamwork. Team meetings, for example, bring employees together to focus upon certain issues. Informing employees about what is happening within the company helps them feel involved and improves their communication.

There are three main methods used for internal communication in the company:

1 written communication

2 electronic communication

3 verbal communication.

Written communication

At Alliance & Leicester written communication is particularly useful when:

- the information needs to be received by many people in different places

- the information needs to be referred to over a period of time.

Written communication in the company includes:

1 *Spectrum* This is a staff newspaper which is distributed to all staff.

2 Team brief This is a monthly production that contains business news from the whole of Alliance & Leicester.

3 Staff suggestion scheme This was created to encourage and reward staff for suggestions. It was also introduced to improve customer service.

4 *Bulletin* Knowledge of product changes and promotional activity is particularly important for staff employed by Alliance & Leicester. The *Bulletin* is produced by the company's Marketing Department to update staff on promotional activity.

5 Office instructions These are paper-based instructions, sent to individual branches, used for updating staff on new product, launches and changes in the business.

6 Office communication These are for branches and usually transmit (send) general messages.

7 One-offs From time to time, one-off communications are produced to update or to emphasise important procedures

Electronic communication

Over recent years there have been many different developments in electronic technology that have affected all staff at Alliance & Leicester in one way or another. Initially the company, like any other business, was dependent on the telephone for internal and external communication.

However, with the recent developments in new technology Alliance & Leicester has invested in new methods of electronic communication:

- e-mail.
- Internet
- fax system
- screen messaging service.

Verbal communication

Verbal communication in the company involves the transmission of information effectively by word of mouth. For many people at Alliance & Leicester, verbal communication tends to be face-to-face messages, personal discussion and the provision of instruction and guidance. However, it also includes staff training sessions, internal conferences, team meetings, videos and audio tapes.

External communication at Alliance & Leicester

The company has a public face or image. This conveys a message that affects everyone who works with the business organisation. These include customers, suppliers, competitors, the government, communities, and agencies.

Methods of external communication include:

1 written communication

2 verbal communication.

Written communication

Alliance & Leicester provides a range of information for different stakeholder groups. In addition to business letters sent to personal customers, written

communications include press releases, advertisements, posters, and mail shots.

Verbal communication

This type of communication is particularly important for a range of issues affecting Alliance & Leicester stakeholders. These include Annual General Meetings, press conferences and 24-hour telephone and postal banking.

 Q 1-5

ACTIVITIES

With your tutor read the above case study carefully and carry out the following activities:

1 Make a list of the different methods of communication that you use to communicate with other students or tutors. For example, writing, asking your tutor questions, etc. Describe the nature and the purpose of each form of communication that you use.

2 Compare and contrast one form of electronic communication with the written communication it was designed to replace.

3 Find out the meaning of the following words:
   a e-mail *letters by internet.*
   b Internet *network, computer.*
   c fax. *letter by phone*

The management of Alliance & Leicester believes that a motivated workforce that feels part of the organisation is the key to achieving its business objectives. Explain how methods of internal communication help the management of Alliance & Leicester to achieve this.

Two-way communications with customers in Alliance & Leicester

As the industry becomes more competitive, using feedback from customers is becoming increasingly important for Alliance & Leicester. Opportunities for two-way communication exist through:

1 Group Customer Relations Customer complaints are a valuable source of information used to improve products and services wherever possible. Customer relations provide a listening ear for customers who are unable to resolve problems with branches. It communicates the feedback to senior management.

2 A Customer Care leaflet This freely available leaflet enables customers to communicate their comments and suggestions to the company.

ACTIVITY

Explain how Alliance & Leicester has effective communication with customers.

Communication technology

Around 50% of Britain's workers are employed in offices. It has been calculated that if all the pieces of paper handled in the world's offices were laid end to end they would stretch from here to the sun! Methods of telecommunication include:

- fax (facsimile) machines
- pagers/bleepers
- mobile phones
- answering machines
- Internet
- teleworking.

ACTIVITIES

I Fill in the gaps in the following statements. Use only one of two words, **written** or **verbal**.
   a Fax is an example of .... communication.
   b Pagers are examples of .... communication.
   c Mobile phones are examples of .... communication.
   d Answering machines are examples of .... communication.
   e The Internet is an example of .... communication.
   f Teleworking is an example of .... communication.

2 Fill in the gaps in the following statements. Use only one term/phrase, **allow(s)** or **do(es) not allow**.
   a Teleworking .... workers and employers to work from home.
   b Fax machines .... documents to be sent quickly from one place to another.

c Mobile phones .... workers to remain in contact with the office wherever they might be.

d Answer machines .... lots of important calls to be missed.

3 Discuss with your tutor whether the following statements are true or false.

a Teleworking reduces costs and reduces travel problems.

b Teleworking increases workers' social isolation.

c Fax machines waste time and delay communication.

d Fax machines increase the reliability and the use of traditional postal services.

e Mobile phones save time and effort.

f Mobile phones reduce the cost of communication.

g Answer machines increase employees' contact with their business.

h Answer machines increase the cost of communication.

Which media of communication?

A number of factors will determine the best choice of medium for any particular message.

A number of questions need to asked:

1 Is the message confidential?
2 Is speed important?
3 Who is to receive the message?
4 Is a permanent record required?
5 Is the message complicated or lengthy?
6 How much will it cost to send the message?

Directions of communication

In any hierarchical structure there are two different directions for formal communication:

1 **Vertical communication** This is the passing of instructions, messages or orders, from managers to employees through the levels of the hierarchy (from top to bottom), for example, between the marketing manager and the marketing team, or passing the information from employees to managers (from bottom to top).

2 **Horizontal communication** This is the type of communication that takes place between people at the same level within the organisation, for example, between the marketing manager and the production manager.

How to write a business letter

Business letters are a very important form of communication. It is essential to know how to communicate in the most effective way. If you are going to write a business

---

Writing a business letter – things to remember

1 Dear Sir or Madam at the beginning of the letter requires 'Yours faithfully' at the end.

2 Dear Mr, Miss, or Mrs at the beginning requires 'Yours sincerely' at the end.

3 The closing paragraph must be a complete sentence. This can be in a number of different forms, for example:

'I look forward to hearing from you' or,

'Please let me know if you require any further information.'

4 When you reply to someone, always start by saying 'Thank you for your letter of (date).'

---

letter, remember the tips in the box (below).

What is a business letter?

A business letter is different from an ordinary letter in the following ways.

- Business letters communicate information between businesses and others, e.g. customers and suppliers. It is important that these letters look good if a business is to give a good impression.
- A business letter is the most frequently used form of external communication for businesses.
- A business letter provides a written record that can be used to send almost any type of information.
- A business letter is usually on headed paper. Fully blocked layout is the most common form of display.

Format of a business letter

There is a basic format that most business letters tend to follow. Quite apart from the style or structure of the letter, the wording

Layout of a business letter

The Design Shop
22 Craft Centre
Deddingham
ML17 9AT

Mrs Smith
18 Meadow Way
Milton Keynes
ML2 1EJ

25 May 2000

Dear Mrs Smith

Order No. 19349 Chrome CD rack

Thanks for your recent order to purchase the above item. We do apologise, as the required item is currently out of stock. However, we promise to do our best to deliver your order in the next two weeks.

Thanks again for your interest in our products.

Yours sincerely,

M Wood

M. Wood

is important. The wording needs to be clear and precise if the message it contains is to be conveyed accurately.

ACTIVITIES

1 Design a suitable letter heading using desktop publishing software for use by:

Light Delight Ltd,
Unit 28, Penraven Industrial Estate,
Mean Wood Road,
Leeds,
LS7 2AP

2 Use your word processing skills to write a letter for the above company from the Production Manager to Speed Supply Ltd of 56 Marton Way, Middlesborough. The out the problems with a new freezer that the company bought 2 months ago. The freezer is still under the supplier's guarantee.

3 Write another letter to Lilter's Electrical Contractors, Grange Street, Leeds, pointing out that their invoice for £83.20 for a replacement light in the marketing department is £15.60 above their original estimate. Would they explain the reason for this?

Memos

Memos are used for internal correspondence/communication between people who work in the same business, usually between managers and employees. Memos are therefore generally less formal than letters in the following ways:

- the business or organisation name does not appear on the memo
- in memos there will be no salutation or complimentary closure such as 'Yours sincerely'
- the memo should be brief and as straightforward as possible
- memos are often distributed to a number of people in the business.

The main uses of memos are:

- the passing of information to people in the business
- requests for information
- confirmation of information, e.g. date of meeting.

ACTIVITY

What are the differences between a memo and a letter?
Fill in the gaps in the following statements using the word memo or letter:

1 A .... is usually shorter than a ....
2 A .... is more formal than a ....
3 A .... is normally initialled, but a .... is signed.
4 A .... is used for internal correspondence but a .... is used for external correspondence.
5 A .... is more confidential than a ....

Unit I Test your knowledge

This is a quick test to help you check how much you have understood.

In the following statements, there are some right and some wrong answers. Circle only the wrong answer/answers:

1 The following are elected management positions:

   a Company secretary
   b Board of directors
   c Sales assistant
   d Managing director

2 The department that has overall responsibility for staff training is:

   a The Human Resources Department
   b The Production Department
   c The Finance Department
   d The Marketing Department

3 The following business ownership has directors:

   a Jones & Partners
   b The Light Delight Ice Cream Ltd
   c Marks and Spencer PLC

4 Advertising is one of the main functions of:

   a The Human Resources Department
   b The Marketing Department
   c The Finance Department
   d The Production Department

5 The purchasing function is sometimes incorporated in:

   a The Marketing Department
   b The Sales Department
   c The Human Resources Department
   d The Production Department

6 The following are the main functions of the Finance Department:

   a Invoicing
   b Payment of wages
   c Balancing the books (accounts)
   d Carrying out market research

7 The following member of Marks & Spencer PLC has overall responsibility for the running of the business:

   a Chairman
   b Managing director
   c Sales manager
   d Sales assistant

8 The following function(s) is/are under the direct control of the Production Department:

   a Stock control
   b Training of staff
   c Advertising
   d Quality control

9 The following products are examples of consumer durables:

   a Ice cream
   b TV
   c Personal computer
   d Dishwasher

10 The following people come at the top level of the hierarchy structure of a large company:

   a Assistant sales manager
   b Marketing director
   c Shareholders
   d Company secretary

11 A long chain of command in a large business leads to:

   a Quicker communication
   b Slow decision making
   c Senior management being close to team workers in the hierarchy structure

12 The statement that includes the required details about a candidate is called:

   a Job description
   b Contract of employment
   c Job specification
   d CV

13 Induction is a type of training that is offered:

   a To any employee in the business
   b To old employees
   c To new employees
   d To senior management

14 The following are the functions of the Human Resources Department:

   a Dealing with resignations
   b Looking after staff welfare
   c Dismissing unsuitable workers
   d Payment of salaries

15 The following is an example of a written method of communication:

   a A letter
   b A memo
   c Telephone
   d Internet

16 The main objective of a business in the public sector is:

   a To make profit
   b To compete
   c To provide a service

17 The following media are examples of external methods of recruitment:

   a Word of mouth
   b Job centres
   c Staff notice board
   d Local newspaper

Unit I Assessment

Check with your tutor what you need to produce for your portfolio. If you do the assignment below, you will be on your way to completing the work you will need to do.

Choose a business either in your area or outside your area. Carry out the following tasks:

1 Draw the organisational chart for this business.
2 Explain the role of each of the following functional areas within the business: Marketing, Finance, Production and Human Resources. Choose one and describe its role in detail, using graphics, if you find this useful.
3 Investigate customer service in the business, and describe how it is carried out.
4 Give full descriptions of two different jobs involving customer service, for example, giving information, helping customers, after-sales service.
5 Evaluate the above two customer service jobs, and suggest how they could be improved.
6 Identify and give examples of types of communication used by the business.
7 Explain how these types of communication serve business activities.
8 Evaluate the above types of communication.

There are many different types of business organisation. This unit will help you to understand the activities that all businesses carry out and how you can identify the differences between them.

In this unit you are going to learn:

- what a business is
- what a business does
- where a business is.

To learn about businesses you have to cover the following topics:

- types of business ownership
- business activities
- people who influence businesses (stakeholders)
- size of business
- businesses location
- business and competition.

When studying businesses it can be useful to group together all businesses that share particular characteristics in order to gain an insight into the problems they face or the advantages they enjoy. Businesses can be classified using three main factors. These factors are:

1 ownership

2 activity

3 scale/size.

Chapter 5 The ownership of businesses

Britain is said to have a mixed economy because it consists of a private sector (privately owned businesses) and a public sector (owned by the government).

In the private sector, decisions about what to produce, how to produce it and where to produce it are made by private individuals. Virtually all businesses in the UK are now in the private sector.

In the public sector, decisions about what to produce, how to produce it and where to produce it are made by central government. The government owns the business.

Private sector ownership

Private sector (enterprise) refers to businesses that are owned by private individuals engaged in the production of goods or services. When you describe a business you must state its type of ownership. In the private sector there are several types of ownership:

* sole trader
* partnership
* private limited company
* public limited company.

There are also two special kinds of ownership in the private sector:

* co-operative
* franchise.

Sole traders

Sole traders are generally small and are often family-run businesses. There is only one owner. He or she has unlimited liability. This means that the owner or 'proprietor' is personally liable for the debts of the business under any circumstances. For example, if the business goes bankrupt, he or she might have to sell personal belongings, such as a car or a house, to pay the debts. There are no particular legal formalities involved in setting up the business apart from those which would apply to any business.

Facts to remember about sole traders:

1 The business is in the private sector.
2 It is easy to set up.
3 There is only one owner.
4 Sole trader runs the business.
5 Sole trader has unlimited liability.
6 Sole trader has full responsibility of running the business.
7 Sole trader makes all the decisions.
8 Business affairs are private.
9 Death or illness of the sole trader could stop the running of the business.

Partnerships

In this type of business there is more than one owner. The control of the business is the responsibility of all the partners. Decisions taken by one partner are binding on the others. Partners have unlimited liability.

A partnership of accountants

Partnerships have a special legal status and are regulated by the Partnership Act of 1890 which allows up to a maximum of 20 partners. Special rules apply to large professional organisations of, for example, accountants and solicitors, where more partners are allowed.

Partnerships are a common type of business and widely used by firms of accountants, doctors, dentists, and other professionals. To avoid any disagreement between partners, it is advisable for a written agreement to be drawn up. This is called a Deed of Partnership.

Facts to remember about a partnership:

1   The business is in the private sector.
2   There can be between 2 and 20 owners.
3   The partners run the business.
4   The partners have unlimited liability.
5   The partners share the responsibility of running the business.
6   The partners share in the decisions.
7   Business affairs are private.
8   Death or illness of a partner does not affect the running of the business.
9   They need a deed of partnership to avoid any arguments.

CASE STUDY – Wild Rice

An idea for a new business can spring out of your daily life. You may notice a problem in getting something you need and then realise that here is a gap in the market that you could fill. That is the way it happened with Margaret.

Nature of business: Producing and supplying pre-packaged vegetarian meals for catering establishments
Location: Glasgow
Business structure: Sole trader (previously partnership)
Proprietor: Margaret Graham

Margaret is a vegetarian. The idea for the business really sprang from when she was going out for a pub lunch. It was very difficult in Glasgow to find vegetarian food in pubs. Margaret and her friend Linda considered various ideas for starting their own business, like a vegetarian restaurant or café. They decided it might be cheaper to set up a small kitchen and supply independent restaurants and pubs with ready-made vegetarian meals.

Market research

Margaret had studied Communications after school, aiming at a career in advertising. The course included market research, so when she and Linda decided to see if they were right about the demand for such meals, her knowledge came in very handy. Margaret and Linda took sample meals to various bars, restaurants, and health food shops, for sample tastings. They also interviewed 100 people for their comments. The feedback was favourable.

'The pub owners were very helpful. They saw that their customers liked our products and, when we told them our prices, they wanted to place orders,' Margaret said.

She continued, 'We went to the local Enterprise Development Unit for advice, and they suggested more market research to be absolutely certain that there was a market. We wrote to Marks and Spencer under the guise of students asking why M&S had started doing vegetarian food and did they see it as a growing field. We also wrote to bookshops and found out that the sale of vegetarian cook books was growing.'

Finance

With no capital of their own, Margaret and Linda had to look for grants. The advice agencies gave them a lot of guidance on this. Glasgow was a development area, so they got a regional development grant.

Also, being under the age of 25 worked in their favour. It enabled them to apply to the Prince's Scottish Youth Business Trust and receive another grant.

Location

Margaret and Linda looked at premises in the city but found nothing suitable that they could afford. Then they came across a huge disused bakery that had been converted into 60 small businesses by a community organisation. It was ideally situated for transport, being near the motorway and the tunnel into the city. It was also outside the city centre, so rates were quite low.

Product

Margaret said, 'Our recipes were adapted from things we made for family and friends. We had to go from making enough for 4 people to making 50 or 60 portions. That was quite difficult to begin with, getting the seasoning right, and the amount of spices and garlic.'

Margaret and Linda cook in bulk, then portion it into individual cardboard dishes. They are sealed in polythene by a machine, then they go into an outer cardboard sleeve printed with their own design. Finally, they are put into large boxes a dozen at a time.

They found that many customers wanted the meals frozen, so they bought a blast-freezer to do this. It also meant they did not have to cook every day.

Customers

Wild Rice has a network of pubs and restaurants in Glasgow and Edinburgh which are supplied either weekly or fortnightly. Orders are taken by telephone. The bulk of customers tend to be small independent grocers and health food shops.

Pricing

Margaret and Linda set prices by taking the costs of the raw materials, electricity, transport and other costs. They also looked at the prices of comparable offerings in the market place, and then discussed matters with business advisers. It was very difficult for them because they knew that if they did not make an income that covered their costs, they would not make any profit.

Margaret is thinking of raising prices slightly because she does not want people to think the products are not very good because they are cheap.

Competition

Wild Rice has competitors such as Birds Eye and Lean Cuisine. However, whereas many companies which sell vegetarian meals tend to just extract meat content from meals, and do not put portions back in, all Wild Rice products are wholefood. They are well balanced, all high in fibre, low in fat, and all the healthy things they should be.

Although it is difficult to compete on advertising with big firms, Margaret and Linda tried to piggy-back on their efforts.

For example, if they saw Lean Cuisine advertising a lot, they would hand out leaflets to their customers.

Business ownership

Margaret and Linda had a partnership agreement drawn up when they started. As it happened they were very close and the partnership was very good. 'As regards dividing up the work, I seemed to be better at the production side of things. Linda was very good on the book-keeping and chasing up payment of accounts,' Margaret said.

Unfortunately, Linda left the business after three years. She had a lot of personal problems. The relationship with her boyfriend broke up and she felt that a lot of it was due to the pressure of being self-employed. 'We got the partnership dissolved (ended) and that was fine. It was very much like a divorce but we were quite happy.'

At first, it was financially and physically difficult for Margaret. She could not prepare the same amount of food that two people could. However, her family was very supportive and she employed a woman who does deliveries and collections three days a week.

Now Margaret is a sole trader and is very happy. In the future, she would like to extend the business further south, down into England. She does not really want to turn the business into a big organisation or huge industry. In fact, she likes the idea that it is small.

ACTIVITY

Read the above case study carefully and answer the following questions:

1 Where did Margaret get her business idea from?
2 Which methods of market research did Margaret use?
3 How did Margaret and Linda manage to obtain money to finance the business?
4 What were the main factors which Margaret and Linda considered in choosing the business location?
5 Explain how the choice of the business premises contributed to the success of the business?
6 Who are Wild Rice's main competitors?
7 How does Wild Rice respond to the competition?
8 Who are Wild Rice's potential customers?
9 What were the main advantages for Margaret of being in a partnership with Linda?
10 What are Wild Rice's main objectives?
11 What are Wild Rice's main business activities?
12 Why do you think Wild Rice is a successful business?
13 Get in touch with the Economic Development Department at your local council. Find out how your local council supports small business in your local area.
14 Margaret is thinking of raising prices slightly. She asks for your advice. Write a short report to advise Margaret what to do.

Limited companies

The main drawbacks of sole trader businesses or partnerships are:

* There is only one or a few owners and they do not have much money to grow or expand.

- The owners have unlimited liability which puts their personal possessions at risk.

Therefore, the need might arise to form a limited company to overcome the two common problems associated with sole traders and partnerships.

The word 'company' suggests a group of owners who have come together to set up a business. In practice, many companies are not like this today because the owners (shareholders) may be quite far removed from the decision-making. Shareholders are rewarded with profit for the risk they take in investing their money into the business. The share of the profit the shareholders receive is called a dividend.

By forming a company, limited liability can be obtained for all members.

Limited liability can be applied to the shareholders of a private or public limited company and partners in a limited partnership.

Facts to remember about a limited company

1 Shareholders are the owners. They invest (put money) into the business.
2 Shareholders are rewarded with profit.
3 Shareholders have limited liability.
4 Shareholders vote for a board of directors.
5 The board of directors runs the company on behalf of the shareholders.
6 Employers are appointed to carry out instructions.

There are two main types of limited companies:

1 private limited company.
2 public limited company.

Setting up a limited company

To set up a limited company (Ltd or PLC), two important documents are needed:

1 Articles of Association
2 Memorandum of Association.

Once these documents are ready, they are sent to someone who is appointed by the Government and called the Registrar of Companies. He or she makes sure that that above two documents are accurate and issues a Certificate of Incorporation which the business needs to start trading.

Private limited company

A private limited company is a limited company in the private sector. Shares are not sold on the Stock Exchange, and shareholders are often made up of family and friends. The company is run by a board of directors who are elected by the shareholders. No minimum (capital) investment is required to set up a private limited company. The minimum number of owners required to set up a private limited company is two. Examples of private limited company are Littlewoods and River Island (which is owned by the Lewis family).

River Island is a private limited company (Ltd)

CASE STUDY — Joseph Dobson & Sons Ltd
Makers of fine quality boiled sweets since 1850

Joseph Dobson & Sons Ltd is one of the largest privately owned confectionery manufacturers in Yorkshire. Dobson's sweets are loved and well stocked in almost all local shops. The advent of the humble polythene bag has enabled the company to increase the distribution of its products more widely and to new outlets such as supermarkets.

The company still runs a traditional sweet shop in Elland, West Yorkshire.

The company is owned and managed by direct descendants of Joseph. The business continued to be passed down from father to son, providing continuity and passing expertise and experience of five generations to the current great-great-grandchild, Miriam, and her husband Stephen.

Dobson & Sons have always been famous for sweets with distinctive flavours and, to add to originality, each type of sweet has its own special shape. Dobson Sweets have always been known as a sweetie manufacturer and the company have always been active in marketing their products at carnival processions, and in mounting displays centred around the giant antique glass jars in shops, supermarkets and museums in the area.

The famous 'Yorkshire Mixtures' sweet was named entirely by accident. The story is that while Joseph's son, Thomas John, was carrying some sweets downstairs, he slipped and the sweets became mixed. Thomas John was inspired to name the jumbled mess "Yorkshire Mixture".

Source: the business website address www.dobsons.co.uk

Read the case study and answer the following questions:

1 What is the type of business ownership for Dobson & Sons?

2 What are the main advantages of this type of ownership?

3 Where did the business name come from?

4 Where is the business located?

5 Where is the business's main market?

6 Where is the product distributed?

7 What is the brand name of Dobson & Sons sweets?

8 Where did the brand name come from?

9 How did the new packaging of the sweets affect sales?

10 Where does the company market the sweets?

11 How has the quality of the sweets contributed to the success of the business?

A private limited company must show the letters Ltd at the end of the company title.

Facts to remember about a private limited company (Ltd)

Many of these facts apply to all limited companies, whether they are private or public. Facts that are only true about private limited companies are highlighted in bold.

1   It is in the private sector.
2   There are two or more owners.
3   Board of directors run the business.
4   Shareholders own the business.
5   Shareholders have limited liability.
6   **No minimum investment.**
7   **Business affairs are private.**
8   Death or illness of shareholders does not affect the running of the business.
9   **Shares are not exchanged or sold on the Stock Exchange.**
10 **Shares are not sold to the general public. They are sold only with the permission of all shareholders, often mainly to family and friends.**

Public limited company

A public limited company (PLC) is a limited company in the public sector. It is owned by shareholders from the public, so shares are sold on the Stock Exchange. The company is run by a board of directors who are elected by shareholders.

Examples of public limited companies are:

* Marks and Spencer PLC
* Barclays Bank PLC
* Halifax PLC.

ACTIVITY

Find out five more examples of public limited companies. You can look at the Stock Market section in a local or a national newspaper.

Facts to remember about a public limited company (PLC)

Many of these facts apply to all limited companies, whether they are public or private. Facts that are only true about public limited companies are highlighted in bold.

1   It is in the private sector.
2   There two or more owners.
3   Board of directors run the business.
4   Shareholders own the business.
5   Shareholders have limited liability.
6   **Minimum investment is £50,000.**
7   **Business affairs are public.**
8   Death or illness of shareholders does not affect the running of the business.
9   **Shares are exchanged or sold on the Stock Exchange.**
10 **Shares are sold to the general public.**

ACTIVITY: PUBLIC OR PRIVATE

Finish off the following statements using only one of the words, **public** or **private**.

1 A sole trader business is in the .... sector.

2 A Ltd company is in the .... sector.

3 For a PLC, business affairs are ....

4 A partnership is in the .... sector.

5 For a sole trader, business affairs are ....

6 A PLC is in the .... sector.

7 For a Ltd company shares are sold in .... to family and friends.

8 For a PLC shares are sold in .... on the Stock Exchange.

CASE STUDY – Chey International

'We are the little fish that swim around amongst the sharks. Anything that is going we take.' That is Chey's comment on how a beginner can move into a field like the rag trade, where struggling small businesses are normal, and still do well.

Nature of business: Manufacturer of leather garments
Location: East End of London
Business ownership: private limited company
Proprietor: Aiyub Ebrahim (nickname Chey)

Chey was born in India but came to Britain when he was 11. He was educated here and went on to university, studying biology. Then he made a basic mistake – he went travelling for about ten years.

'I did odd jobs to survive – everything you can think of, from dish-washing upwards. Then I decided to do something more positive. It is pure coincidence I ended up in this business', Chey said.

He knew a friend who wanted some CMT work done. CMT is contract work in the clothing industry. The major wholesalers gave Chey the materials and he just made it up. They paid him for the labour charges, so he did not need capital to start.

Location

Chey saw some premises that were empty, got second-hand sewing machines and recruited a few machinists from amongst people he knew.

Chey's father was a tailor, so he had some background in the rag trade. Chey himself had no personal experience of the industry, he just picked it up as he went along. 'My goal was to make as much money as possible and get out. I planned to work all hours of the day, get the money, get back to Germany and open a shop.'

Chey opened a leather shop in Munich in Germany, but unfortunately that failed. He had to come back to Britain and the firm has been going now for four years.

'With contract work, everything is done for you – all the designing, all the selling, you just supply the labour.' It took Chey a year or two to learn the tricks of the trade. Chey International Ltd became the King of the CMT trade for a time. Wholesalers were chasing them to make up garments for them.

It did not take Chey long to realise this was a mugs' game. It was the wholesalers who decided which firms they would give work to and how much they would pay. The flow of work could suddenly stop or reduce to a trickle that was not enough to survive. They were not really concerned to pay good enough rates to develop their suppliers to a level where they would be stable.

The wholesalers were keen to pay as little as possible, so that the percentage they added on when selling to the stores could be as high as possible.

Therefore, Chey thought if he could sell directly to the stores, he could offer a lower price and still make enough profit to pay his employees.

Chey's company has now reached the stage where they do not do CMT work any more. They make their own garments. Chey has a friend who does the designing and the sales. He goes to the shops and takes the concept he has designed. He explains, 'We can make anything you want exclusive to you, all you have to do is to tell us what you want.' So the customer gets a better service.

Chey's company can make better products and more quickly. For example, if a shop phones up and says 'I want 50 jackets' the business can produce them in two days. The big wholesaler wants at least six weeks.

Competition

Chey International can also react to changes in fashion, whereas the big firms cannot. They import most of their materials from the Far East. They have to place big orders months in advance, and take the risk that changing fashion will make it unsaleable.

However, Chey recognises the danger in taking business from under the wholesalers' noses. If he grows too big he feels they will cut their prices to a very low level to drive him out of the market. That is why he tends to stay clear of the big department stores which are the wholesalers' major customers.

How the company is run

On friendly terms with all employees, Chey believes in being closely involved in the work. He has done most of the tasks himself, except the machining. He usually inspects the finished garments, ensuring they are up to the quality he wants.

Chey admits to being a workaholic, with little relaxation apart from watching videos when he gets home in the evenings. Now the company has reached a more stable level and can take on specialists to handle different aspects of management, Chey feels he may be able to take a bit more time for himself.

Read the case study carefully and answer the following questions:

1   What type of company ownership is Chey International?
2   What are the main advantages of this type of ownership?
3   Who are the owners of the business in this type of ownership?
4   What are Chey's main personal skills which contributed to the success of his business?
5   What are Chey International's main business activities?
6   Chey said that the attitude of wholesalers put him in a 'mugs game'. Explain what he meant.
7   Who are Chey's main customers?
8   Who are Chey's main competitors?
9   How does Chey respond to the competition?
10 Who are the stakeholders who influence Chey International's activities?

Co-operatives

Co-operatives are a special type of ownership in the private sector.

How co-operatives developed

People organising themselves together as a co-operative is not a new idea. It dates back several hundred years in many areas of the world, although we usually think of the Co-op Movement in this country developing from the 19th century. It was a time of rapid industrialisation, low wages and poor living conditions. Therefore, the consumer co-operatives were set up by the Rochdale Pioneers to provide a cheap source of food for themselves. Around the same time, the first worker co-operatives were established.

There are several different types of co-operatives which share the same basic principles of:

- democratic control
- ownership by members.

The most popular co-operative in the United Kingdom is the Co-operative Wholesale Society (CWS). It is the modern successor of the co-operative movement founded in Rochdale in 1844.

Co-Op is Britain's best known co-operative business

Facts to remember about a co-operative

1 A co-operative is in the private sector.
2 A co-operative is a special type of ownership.
3 There are many types of co-operative, e.g. consumer co-operative, worker co-operative and producer co-operative.
4 The most common type of co-operative is a worker co-operative, where workers run and own the business.

Co-operatives and the law

Businesses can register as co-operative societies under the Industrial and Provident Societies Acts of 1965-1975. The Co-operative Development Agency (CDA) and the Industrial Common Ownership Movement (ICOM) assist with the setting up of co-operatives; for example, by providing advice, training and business information.

ACTIVITY: WHO ARE THE OWNERS?

The main principle of co-operatives is that members have a democratic say and control over the business.
Read the above information carefully.
Fill in the gaps in the following sentences, stating who are the owners and who are the runners in each type of the following co-ops.

1 In a consumer co-operative .... own the business and .... run the business.
2 In a worker co-operative .... own the business and .... run the business.
3 In a producer co-operative .... own the business and .... run the business.
4 In a retailer co-operative .... own the business and .... run the business.

CASE STUDY – Speedy M & V

A good basis for your own business is often the skills and experience you have acquired in your paid employment. That was what Monica and Violet decided, but they didn't like the idea of being bosses. In preparing for the future when they expected their business to expand, they opted for a co-operative structure rather than that of a partnership.

If you would like to know why, read the following case study.

Nature of business: Word processing/typing bureau
Location: Central London
Business ownership: co-operative
Proprietors: Monica Butcher and Violet Fearon

Violet did secretarial training after school and worked as a secretary for various companies. When she joined an insurance company in the City, she met Monica Butcher. They became friends and discussed the idea of starting their own business. They liked the idea of working for themselves.

In the next few years, Violet did a three-year course in Business Studies at a Technical College and Monica took a short business course. Finding time to plan your own business project properly can be a problem. Violet's course helped there. 'At the end of my course, we had to do a project about starting our own business and mine was about starting a secretarial agency.'

Type of business ownership

Monica and Violet went on a weekend course at the City University about small businesses. Different business structures were discussed. They liked the sound of a co-operative. It seemed to offer the possibility of financial and other assistance, and everybody is equal in a co-op.

Monica and Violet then went to Islington Co-operative Development Agency (one of the many CDAs around the country). There they were helped to write a business plan and a cash flow forecast over three years.

Setting up a co-operative

Monica and Violet registered through ICOM (Industrial Common Ownership Movement Ltd) and they liaised with Companies House on the Memorandum and Articles of Association. That is the formal document needed to register as a company limited by guarantee, one of the ways becoming a co-operative.

Market research

Monica and Violet carried out market research to find out how easy it would be to get customers. They drew up a questionnaire, and telephoned firms from the *Yellow Pages*.

Finance

The CDA suggested that they should apply to Islington Council's Economic Development Unit for a grant. 'They were keen on supporting co-ops,' explained Monica.

Premises

The next step was finding premises. Monica and Violet went to estate agents, and to the Council which had a list of vacant business properties. They chose premises which were near to the City of London and all those potential customers.

Speedy M & V has its office on a busy road on the first floor over a bookmaker's. The main office has enough space to add more desks and equipment, if required. It also has a small kitchen and toilet and a separate reception area.

Monica and Violet worked very long hours during the week and sometimes they came in on Saturdays to finish a rush job.

There were bad weeks too, with only one or two jobs. The work consists mostly of letters and reports for companies, theses for students at the nearby university, copy typing, audio typing and typing up accounts.

Promotion

To get customers when they started Monica and Violet promoted their business in different ways:

1 They printed leaflets and business cards which they designed themselves.
2 They did a mailshot with the leaflets – went around putting leaflets through the letter boxes of local firms.
3 They put a small advertisement in the local newspaper, which produced the best results.
4 They put business cards up on notice boards in the university.

'Speedy M & V'

For all your word processing and typing needs

All jobs considered – large or small

1 The Elm Trees
Oxford
OX2 6BP

---

5 They advertised in the *Yellow Pages*, the local telephone directory and business directories.
6 They also made a point each morning, when they were not too busy, of selecting 10 companies each from the *Yellow Pages* and ringing them up.

Business future

Violet does the book keeping and they both do invoicing. They split all the other tasks between them. They also have a management meeting, just the two of them, to discuss what order to tackle the jobs in.

Monica and Violet are now getting to the stage where they have to submit the annual accounts for the first year. Therefore, they are looking for an accountant to audit those.

The current debate is whether they can buy more equipment and afford to start doing desktop publishing.

They also see themselves expanding into photocopying, and recruitment. Of course, it would take more people to handle all that, so they would have to take other people into the co-operative as equals.

Monica and Violet still keep in touch with the CDA. They tell them how they are doing and the CDA has helped them with tax problems, cashflow forecasts and with getting rate reductions.

Monica and Violet are now well into their second year. They have needed most of the income from the business to buy extra bits of equipment and furniture. They are much happier than being employed as secretaries by a company.

Read the above case study carefully and answer the following questions:

1 Why did Monica and Violet choose a co-operative type of ownership?
2 What are the disadvantages of this type of ownership?
3 How did Monica and Violet manage to raise money (finance) for their business?
4 What are Speedy M & V's main objectives?
5 How did the government help Monica and Violet?
6 In which industrial sector does Speedy M & V operate?
7 Get in touch with the Economic Development Department in your local council. Find out examples of co-operatives in your local area.

Franchise

Franchising is a type of business ownership which allows the owners to enjoy the benefits of running their own business without the risk of failure.

How does it work?

- In franchising, a big company, such as Kentucky Fried Chicken or Body Shop, allows someone to buy the right to use their products or techniques under their trade name.
- Franchising offers a 'ready-made' business opportunity for those who have the capital and are willing to work hard.
- Franchising is one of the fastest growing sectors of the economy and accounts for 20 per cent of retail sales.

Public sector ownership

The UK has a mixed economy. This means that, as well as many businesses being privately owned, there are others which are run by the government. These government-run enterprises make up what is known as the public sector. The public sector is made up of government departments (e.g. The Department of Education) and local council services (e.g. libraries and sport centres).

The public sector offers many goods and services to consumers. Some of these goods and services are financed entirely by money the government obtains from taxes or by borrowing (e.g. Education or National Health Service). They are offered to the consumer free of direct charge at the point of use.

The government produces goods and services that it is believed the private sector cannot or will not produce efficiently.

Facts to remember about a franchise

1 A franchise business is in the private sector.
2 A franchise business is a special type of ownership.
3 The franchisee could be a sole trader, partnership or a company.
4 The franchisee is the person or business which buys a ready made business name
5 The franchiser is the person, business who sells a ready business name.
6 The franchisee pays the franchiser a sum of money to buy the business name.
7 The franchiser offers advice and training to the franchisee.
8 The franchisee pays a share of the profit at the end of the year to the franchiser.

Why a public corporation?

There are number of reasons why public corporations have been set up:

1 To avoid waste of resources and confusion. For example, just imagine if more than one bank was allowed to print notes and coins in England and Wales!!

2 To protect jobs and key industries. Many people feel that the government has a responsibility to protect jobs, even if this means lower profits, for example, in the mining industry.

3 To set up and run important but non-profitable services. For example, although the BBC makes sure that most of its programmes are profitable and popular, it also operates a loss-making service in some areas, for example, producing special programmes for minority groups.

The BBC is a public corporation

Facts to remember about a public corporation
1 It is in the public sector.
2 It is owned by the government.
3 It is controlled by the government.
4 It is run by a board of directors.
5 It provides a service to the national economy.
6 It protects jobs.

ACTIVITY

Find out examples of businesses which are owned by the local council in your area. You might need to ring the Economic Development Department in your local council.

ACTIVITY: WHAT IS THE TYPE OF OWNERSHIP?

Find out the type of ownership for each of the following businesses. Choose one of the following: sole trader, Limited Company, partnership, franchise, PLC, co-operative.

1 Keith Ellis owns a plumbing business called 'Quality Plumbing, Bathrooms and Tiling'. The business was established 21 years ago and offers 24-hour service. Keith makes all the business decisions and takes all the profit. However, everything he owns is at risk.

2 James and Asif own 'Happy Motoring Garage'. They have owned the business for 13 years. James and Asif know that if the business does not succeed everything they own is at risk. Therefore, although they employ 7 mechanics to work for them,

they run the business themselves, and make all the decisions. The business is going from strength to strength and James and Asif enjoy sharing the profit.

3 Smith Gordon and Sons is a removal business. It is a family business which was established in 1958 and since then it has been run and owned only by the Gordon family. Robert Gordon is the managing director and has shares in the business. There are also another four managers.

4 The Golden Arms Co, Ltd provides training. The Carter family take 15% of the profit every year.

5 Global Telecom is a large company which operates in the communication and telecommunication sector. The company is owned by hundreds of shareholders who share the business profit at the end of each year.

Business size (scale)

The European Commission has introduced one method of defining business size by numbers employed. For example:

Micro	1–5 employees
Small	6–99 employees
Medium	100–250 employees
Large	250+ employees

The market share of a business is its total sales as a percentage of the total sales of the industry in which it operates. For example, Marks & Spencer holds 15% of the UK clothing market.

It is important to point out that if a business employs fewer than 100 people, but has a 90 per cent share of the market in which it operates, the influence it exerts on that market will be greater than the influence exerted on its market by a business employing thousands, whose market share is only 20 per cent.

Some businesses can never grow very large because their market is small or geographically limited. Craft or luxury goods producers cannot become mass producers or they lose the essential features of their production. For example, Rolls-Royce cars, which are still partly hand made, remains a very small company when compared to Ford or Nissan.

Key Terms

Articles of Association One of the legal documents that the Registrar of Companies requires for the setting up of a company. It contains the day-to-day rules about how the company will operate and how the shareholders will be involved in the business.

Certificate of Incorporation A certificate issued by the UK Registrar of Companies at the stage of setting up a business when all the other required documents have been drawn up and registered.

Competition The idea that in a market one producer should always be rivalled by another producer to ensure that prices are kept low and the customer is not exploited.

Consumer A person who buys goods and services for his or her own use or consumption.

Deed of partnership The legal contract which controls how a partnership will be owned and organised.

Franchise A special type of ownership in the private sector, where a franchisee (a person or a business) buys a ready made business name/opportunity from a franchiser, such as McDonald's or Pizza Hut.

Franchisee The business or person that buys a franchise (a ready made business name or opportunity) from a franchiser.

Franchiser The business or person that sells a ready made business name or opportunity, e.g. Kentucky Fried Chicken and Body Shop.

Limited company A registered company where the liability of its members is restricted to the amount of capital they have put into the business.

Limited liability The owners of a company are liable for only the amount of capital that they have put into a company in the event of that company being wound up.

Memorandum of Association One of the documents that the owners of a company have to place with the Registrar of Companies when the company is formed. It contains the external affairs of the business, i.e. address, name, capital raised.

Mixed economy In this type of economy the government and the private sector share the ownership of resources. In a mixed economy, as in the UK, there is a private and a public sector.

Objective The particular goal that an organisation is trying to achieve.

Partnership A type of legal organisation for a business which has between two and twenty owners, and each partner has unlimited liability.

Private limited company A limited company that does not issue shares for public sale and its shares cannot be sold or transferred in the Stock Exchange, for example, Littlewoods.

Private sector That part of a mixed economy in which decisions about what to produce, how to produce it and where to produce it are made by private individuals. Virtually all businesses in the UK are now in the private sector.

Profit It is what the business has left after it has paid all the costs of producing its goods and services.

Public corporation A limited company which is owned by the government and is in the public sector, for example the BBC. A public corporation is run by a board of directors.

Public limited company (PLC) A form of limited company where that public are invited to buy shares on the Stock Exchange. Two people are the minimum number needed to set up a PLC, for example, Halifax PLC.

Public sector That part of a mixed economy where decisions about what to produce, how to produce it and where to produce it, are made by central government rather than being left to private individuals.

Public services Those services which are provided by the state, either free of charge or below the market price, to all members of the public, for example, the National Health Service.

Registrar of Companies The government official who is responsible for recording details of companies established in the UK.

Risk All business decisions involve an element of risk because there are a number of possible outcomes from a decision.

Scale The size of a business, which is sometimes measured by the number of people who work in the business.

Sales income The money that a business receives as a result of selling its products.

Sole trader A type of business organisation where one person is the owner and where that person has sole responsibility for the decisions in the business. He or she has unlimited liability.

Stock Exchange It is the place where buyers and sellers trade in shares, for example, London Stock Exchange.

Unlimited liability A form of liability in which the owners of a business are personally responsible for all the losses of the business, irrespective of the amount of capital they have invested in it, i.e. sole trade or partnership.

Chapter 6 Business activities

Introduction

Every business will have a key activity. Body Shop develops and sells beauty products. Even within an organisation as diverse as Richard Branson's Virgin (from airlines to soft drinks), there will be different divisions with their own focus. Someone working in the Cola part of the business will not be involved in developing financial services.

When you collect your evidence for this unit for your portfolio it is very important

that you choose two contrasting (different) organisations. The pages that follow describe different types of business activity and will help you understand your chosen organisation.

Business organisations can be classified according to their production activity into three main sectors:

- primary sector
- secondary sector
- tertiary sector.

CASE STUDY – Boots Contract Manufacturing

Boots Contract Manufacturing (BCM) develops and manufactures a wide range of quality cosmetics and toiletry products. It is the largest contract manufacturer in Europe. It manufactures over 450 million units and produces over 4500 different products a year. The main product ranges are:

- over-the-counter medicines
- prescription medicine
- colour cosmetics
- suncare
- baby toiletries
- skincare
- haircare and styling
- vitamins
- oral hygiene.

BCM has seven factories and one major development laboratory. These are located on the company's main site at Nottingham and in Airdrie, Scotland.

Read the above case study carefully and answer the following questions:

1   What are the main advantages for BCM of producing more than one product?

2   In which industrial sector does BCM operate?

3   In which side of manufacturing is BCM specialised?

4   Find another 5 examples of manufacturing businesses or companies. You might find the information in the *Yellow Pages* or your local library.

Primary sector

The primary sector is concerned with the extraction (digging out) of basic raw materials provided by nature which are either above or below the earth's surface. Examples are farming, fishing and mining.

Secondary sector

The secondary sector consists of the manufacturing and construction industries; These products include: capital goods (goods purchased by businesses to make other products, e.g. a car manufacturer needs to buy metal products in order to be able to make cars); and consumer goods (products which you can buy in high-street shops). Raw materials are made into end products.

Tertiary sector

The tertiary sector is also called the service sector. The service sector includes retailing (selling clothes, food, furniture, computers etc), leisure and entertainment (cinemas, clubs, theme parks, hairdressers etc),

CASE STUDY – Northern Foods PLC

Northern Foods PLC is a leading UK food producer, focused on two distinct operating areas:

1 chilled foods
2 convenience foods.

Their Prepared Foods business is Britain's foremost supplier of high quality chilled foods under their own labels or those of major retailers. The company also has a strong branded presence in biscuits, fresh chilled dairy products, frozen food and savoury pastry products. The business brands which include Fox's, Ski, Goodfella's and Pork Farms, account for one-third of their sales.

The business has a very strong and competitive position in all markets, based on a consistent investment in high quality, low cost production facilities.

The company also owns the Smiths Flour Mills, which has five mills supplying wheat and other flours to Northern Foods companies and food manufacturers.

Read carefully the case study and answer the following questions:

Examples of some of the branded foods Northern Foods PLC makes

1 What are Northern Foods PLC's main business activities?
2 Which business activities take part in the primary sector?
3 How important are primary sector activities for the business?
4 Which business activities take part in the secondary sector?
5 Which business activities take part in

activities such as banking and insurance and public services such as education, the police and the fire service.

ACTIVITY

In your groups, identify three businesses in the primary sector, three businesses in the secondary sector, and three businesses in the tertiary sector. You can use the *Yellow Pages* to help you to find out about businesses.

ACTIVITY: WORKFORCE IN THE INDUSTRIAL SECTORS

1 Make a list of the occupations of 15 adults who are known to you (members of your family or neighbours).
2 With your tutor, decide how many of the 15 belong to the primary, secondary and tertiary sectors.
3 Present the numbers of the adults working in different sectors in a spreadsheet.
4 Combine your totals with those of other members of the group.
5 Draw a diagram or bar chart to present the percentage of people working in each sector.
6 How do you think this diagram might look in 50 years' time?

Wholesale activities

A wholesaler is the person or business which is the middle person between the manufacturer and the retailer. The wholesaler buys goods from a manufacturer in bulk to sell on to retailers.

A manufacturer will normally seek the services of wholesalers. They carry the cost of storing goods and transporting them to the final customer. The wholesalers bear some of the risk of non-payment which a manufacturer might otherwise run. The wholesaler has to pay the manufacturer of the goods and then try to get the money back when the goods are re-sold. The wholesaler may make a loss if the goods involved go out of fashion. As well as advising retailers about new products, the wholesaler will inform the manufacturer of changes in taste and demand by adjusting their own purchases.

There has been a growth of wholesalers which sell direct to the general public. These large discount stores sell furniture and other household products with relatively poor customer facilities. This is often the case for building materials or consumer durable goods such as furniture.

Wholesales markets exist throughout the country where goods such as meat, fruit and

Smithfield's Market is a wholesale meat market

fish are sold in the very early hours of the morning. The most popular wholesale markets are:

- Meat – Smithfields Market, London
- Fish – North Quay, Isle of Dogs, London
- Fruit- Nine Elms, London.

Despite the advantages of the wholesale service, the manufacturer may not use it if it believes it is possible to provide the same service itself at cheaper prices.

ACTIVITY

1 What are the advantages of wholesaler services for manufacturer and customers?
2 Find out five examples of wholesalers in your local area.
3 Find out on which day in your local area the wholesale market for fish or fruit takes place.

Other service activities

Services are the commercial activities that assist trade in its job of selling goods and services. Examples include banking, finance, insurance and transport. Financial services now account for one-fifth and services in general for two-thirds of all UK output.

Banking services

Commercial or 'high street' banks such as Barclays, Lloyds TSB and NatWest, are public limited companies, and one of the institutions which provide business capital. They can offer both long-term capital, in terms of loans and mortgages, and short-term loans, for example, overdrafts. The commercial banks also provide a wide range of other services to businesses.

The main business activity of a bank is to provide a service

Healthcare services

Some businesses exist mainly to provide healthcare services to customers. You learned early on in this unit in chapter 5 that the public sector is made up of public corporations, nationalised industries, central government departments (e.g., Department of Health) and local government services (e.g., council-run leisure centres). The main aim here is not to make profit, but to provide a service for the community.

The UK healthcare service is provided mainly by the government, and called the National Health Service. It is paid for through taxes and national insurance contributions. Many organisations work together to provide the total service, for example, hospitals, family planning clinics, and General Practitioner Clinics (GPs).

However, there are still healthcare services on a smaller scale which are provided by the private sector, for example, BUPA.

ACTIVITIES

1 Look in the *Yellow Pages* (under the hospital and clinic sections) for the list of organisations which provide healthcare services to the local community in your area.
2 Find out how many private hospitals there are in your local area which provide private healthcare services.
3 Interview 10 of your friends, neighbours or relatives to ask them about their views on the healthcare service they get.
   a How many of them have private health insurance?
   b What are their views about the quality of the services which are provided by the National Health Service?
4 Collect a leaflet from one of the private hospitals in your local area. Check what services it offers and how much they cost.

Leisure and sport

Some businesses are mainly set up to provide leisure and/or sports services. Stadiums and leisure centres are mainly owned by the local council to provide these services for the local community.

Charity activities

Charities are part of what is called the voluntary sector. Their purpose is very different from most other private sector organisations. They exist to promote and support a cause or activity and, as such, do not have a profit motive. This is not to say that they do not make profits. In fact, many charities have subsidiaries that sell goods or services but their profits are re-invested to support the main charitable aim.

ACTIVITIES

1 Collect an article which describes a charitable event in your local area. Find out who organised the event and what the main purpose was.
2 Visit your local library and find out the addresses of the charitable organisations in your local area.

Transport activities

Businesses use transport to distribute their products to customers. Whether the manufacturers deliver products to wholesalers, retailers or directly to customers, they need some sort of transport. Therefore, all businesses one way or another have transport activities as part of their trading activities.

There are a number of conflicting pressures on a firm when it comes to choosing how to deliver or distribute its product to customers. Final decisions will be based on the:

- cost of transport
- type of market
- type and the image of the product.

The cost of transport depends on the method of transport to be used. In choosing which method of transport to use a firm must consider the cost, urgency, distance, the product, and the safety and security of this product.

Once again the firm is faced with a range of conflicting pressures when making its choice. For example, the safest method of transport might be too slow or too

(contd. on page 80)

C A S E   S T U D Y — Calles and Cakes

Maggie Smith and Joan Curtis design and make cakes for special occasions such as weddings and birthdays. Their business is run from Maggie's home. They spend a lot of time in the kitchen, baking and decorating, but they also have to order and collect the ingredients, keep accounts and deliver the finished cakes to customers.

Until a few months ago, most of their business came from family and friends. However, when they started advertising in the local paper, the orders came flooding in, mainly by telephone. They also received an offer from a top department store for them to supply 'designer' cakes for their customers.

Joan and Maggie were delighted that their business was growing but it gave them a problem. With all the increased orders they were, inevitably, spending more time out and about. They realised that they could lose customers, or potential customers, who rang and found the phone unanswered or engaged. Their families were out at work or school all day, so they couldn't help. Their income, although growing, would not stretch to employing staff. They had to rethink their communications needs. They found some simple and inexpensive solutions:

1 installing telephone extensions into Maggie's kitchen and into her spare room which doubles as their office
2 having a telephone in the kitchen with a memory to store numbers which they ring regularly

3 having a telephone answering machine which picks up calls whilst they are out or too busy to answer the phone
4 making use of relatively new telephone network services, 'Call waiting' and 'Call diversion'.

Read the above case study carefully and answer the following questions:

1 How can the new telecommunication techniques help Maggie and Joan to run the business?
2 Find out from your local BT shop the services which each of the above telecommunication options can provide Maggie and Joan.
3 How do you think this could help their business?
4 What other telecommunication solutions can Maggie and Joan use for their business?

expensive. In a business operating for profit the main consideration will usually be to keep costs as low as possible.

ACTIVITY: WHICH METHOD OF TRANSPORT?

1 Sort out the following methods of transport, starting with the most expensive one first: road transport, rail transport, sea transport, air transport, inland waterway.
2 Suggest the best method (quickest, safest, cheapest) method to transport the following products:
   - oil and gas
   - timber or coal
   - fresh flowers
   - bricks

- fleet of cars
- fresh bread.

Communication and telecommunication

Some businesses specialise in communication and telecommunication products and services. For example, CableTel and BT are the most popular businesses in this sector. The two companies are in competition and each of them is trying to attract more customers.

Communications are becoming increasingly important in our modern life. With a fast style of life and people becoming more time-conscious, the use of communication services and products is increasing rapidly. For example, the mobile phone market is growing rapidly and prices are becoming lower and more affordable.

CASE STUDY – In touch with BT

'Keeping in touch has always been our business at BT. That, after all, is what telephone networks are made for. But to our mind, there is much more to it than giving you a fast and simple way of contacting your family and friends. We constantly provide our customers with the latest communication products and services. Telephones and answer machines with the latest technology, fax machines and mobile phones are examples of our communication products. Our network service includes high quality services which BT provides to customers, for example, Call Waiting, Call Diversion, Three Way Calls and Call Reminders, etc. But the improvements to our communication service don't end there. We also recognise that we need to be in touch with what customers want from us.'

Read carefully the above case study about BT and answer the following questions:

1 What are the main communication activities for BT?
2 Who are BT's main competitors?
3 What other communication services does BT offer? You can get in touch with your local BT shop or ring 0800 622302 to find more information about BT communication products.
4 Find from the *Yellow Pages* other businesses which operate in the communication sector. Make a list of them.

Key Terms

Charities Any of the organisations, such as those often found in the voluntary sector of an economy, for example, Oxfam. They exist to promote and support a cause or activity and, as such, do not have a profit motive.

Consumer A person who buys goods and services for his or her own use or consumption.

Goods A general term used for the wide variety of visible items which are produced by a business, e.g. cars, computers etc.

Primary production The stage of economic activity that involves the extraction of natural resources from the land so that they can be used in the secondary stage of production, for example, mining, farming and fishing.

Production Describes the way a business uses financial and human resources to make raw materials into an end product that is consumed by someone else.

Recession Period of time when the economy is slowing down or output is falling.

Retailing The last stage in the channel of distribution which involves the final selling to consumers of the goods and services that have been produced.

Secondary production The manufacturing of products from raw materials or other manufactured products, for example, wood into tables.

Service A term used to describe invisible items, such as banking, insurance, education, which are provided by a business or person.

Tertiary production The provision of services which help to support the other two sectors of economic activity, the primary and the secondary sectors. It includes professional services, administration transport, banking, insurance and the public services, including health and education.

Wholesaler The middle person between producers and consumers. The wholesaler plays the important role of breaking down the bulk of what is produced by the manufacturer, and delivering the goods in smaller quantities to retailers which then sell them to customers.

Chapter 7 The location of businesses

No matter where you live in Britain it is extremely probable that the type of industries in your area have changed considerably over the last 50 years. Traditionally, the North of England was renowned for the heavy industries: steel, ship building, coal mining, and for cotton and wool manufacture. The Midlands were famous for car production, pottery and engineering. The South East had a range of manufacturing companies plus canneries, refineries, tobacco companies and warehouses near the docks. Cornwall and South Wales were mining communities, the first for tin and the second for coal.

Current industrial trends

The trend today is for newer industries to emerge, for example, in computers and electronics, light engineering and telecommunications, together with a growth in the service industry.

Automation (the use of modern technology) has reduced the number of people employed and the size of factories and in nearly all areas industries have moved out of town and inner city areas to new industrial areas and parks on the outskirts – away from residential areas.

Factors affecting location

One of the earliest decisions any entrepreneur (owner) has to make is where to locate his or her business in order to be successful. To do this, he or she has to make a careful assessment of costs. The ideal location would be the one where costs are minimised. The entrepreneur would need to look at the benefits which each area has to offer as well as any government help which might be available.

Factors affecting the location of a business can be divided into three main areas:

* costs of location
* benefits of location
* government influence on location (help and constraints).

Costs and benefits affecting location

For every potential site, the business needs to look at a combination of factors to weigh up the advantages and disadvantages of each. The site chosen will be the one that provides the best overall result, and not necessarily the best in every category. All of the factors which are going to be mentioned below have to be considered, assessed and ranked in order of importance to make the final choice about where to locate the business.

I The need to be close to customers

The market is made up of the customers of a particular product or service. The market will almost always be a crucial factor in deciding location. Service industries (such as shops) need to locate near their customers, and large shopping centres need to locate near to major centres of population. For example, the Metro Centre outside Newcastle and Meadowhall outside Sheffield are both located near large cities and the motorway network.

Meadowhall, Sheffield, is conveniently located near the motorway

2 Nearness to raw materials and natural resources

Businesses in the primary sector generally need to be close to the natural resources which they use, for example, coal mining in Yorkshire, quarrying in North Wales. Likewise, fishing and forestry can take place only near their raw materials. The primary sector includes farming which takes place where there is arable or grazing land for crops or livestock.

Businesses in the secondary sector, i.e. manufacturers, sometimes locate near their raw materials or near the ports through which the raw materials are imported. This is especially true when the raw materials are bulky and, therefore, expensive to transport. For example, Britain's steel industry was located in towns such as Scunthorpe because these places are close to the iron ore which is an essential ingredient of steel production. Businesses which need to be located near the raw materials they use are known as bulk-decreasing industry. This is because the raw materials are bulky but the final product is not. Bulk-increasing industries, on the other hand, need to be located near their markets, because their final product is either bulky or fragile.

3 Transport costs

Different industries have different transport needs. Two major influences are the pull of the market and of the raw material. These depend on whether the industry is bulk increasing or bulk decreasing. However, many industries' markets are spread out and raw materials come from several suppliers, for example, the car industry.

4 Land costs

Land costs vary considerably nationally and some firms might need a large square footage. They might, therefore, be influenced by the cheaper rents and property prices found in some areas. For example, the cost of land is higher in the South of England than in the North.

5 Cost of premises

Firms generally need to buy or hire premises on which to carry out their business. Shops will pay high rents for premises only if the location brings sufficient revenue. For example, a jewellers' shop might be profitable enough to be sited on a town's most expensive street, but a less profitable store selling second-hand motor parts probably could not afford such a site.

6 Supply of skilled and experienced labour

The availability of labour might attract firms to an area, particularly if that labour force has the skills the firms require. Increasingly, a key factor for many businesses is the availability of a supply of labour that is skilful and experienced. It is important for a company to know that it will be able to employ workers who are capable and competent. For example, there is no point in McDonald's opening a new restaurant in an area where there is a shortage of people available to work in the business.

Certain areas have colleges which offer training specifically for local industry, for example, agricultural colleges in rural areas that specialise in farming, or engineering courses in colleges near manufacturing plants.

7 Safety

Some industries have to locate their premises well away from high density population levels and their location is limited, for example, nuclear power industries.

8 Waste disposal

Certain industries produce considerable waste and the costs associated with the disposal of this might affect location. Some plants are on rivers or the coast so that waste products such as hot water can be pumped away. Also, large chemical plants and nuclear power stations are sited away from towns and cities so that, if there is an accident, fewer people will be affected.

9 Communication

The accessibility of motorways, ports and airports have become increasingly important locational factors over recent years. A sound infrastructure (the term is used for network, bridges, building, motorway) creates the opportunity to trade with ease, for example, South East England.

In the last century many businesses located near the railways for the same reason. Some specialist companies which produce small, expensive goods with a worldwide market locate near airports.

10 Regional advantages

A number of facilities for certain industries might be concentrated in particular regions. A concentration of similar industries and subsidiary industries could well attract a firm, as could skilled labour, local research facilities and commercial markets.

11 Government influence

In the UK, some areas have higher levels of unemployment than others. The main reason the government may wish to influence the location of industry is to improve the regional balance of employment; in other words, to move production into regions of high unemployment and areas where industry has declined. These areas of the country, such as Newcastle (its shipbuilding industry declined, creating high unemployment), receive investment aid from the UK government and from the EU.

The government also restricts the areas where businesses may locate in order to protect the environment.

12 History and tradition

Some businesses are located where they are because they have a long tradition of being in that place. For example, some of the finest makers of quality pottery, such as

Wedgwood, have always been located in Staffordshire. This has meant that the name Staffordshire itself has come to be associated with quality pottery. Also, the fact that pottery has been made in this area for a long time means that there is a good supply of people with the sorts of skills needed to work in this industry. Therefore, a pottery business located in Staffordshire would probably be reluctant to move from the area, and the owners of a new pottery business might be attracted to locate their business there.

Other factors affecting location

1 The personal preference of the owner

In some cases, the personal decision of the owner will be the deciding factor. It is said that Detroit became the motor car capital of the USA because Henry Ford chose to live near there. This factor can be equally important if a location has a negative image, i.e. depressed and contain declining industries. In this case, owners of new businesses might not wish to locate there.

2 The location of other businesses

In some cases, such as shoe shops and estate agents, businesses cluster together because customers 'shop round'. Any shop or business not near the others will be at a disadvantage because most potential customers will visit only the main cluster. On the other hand, businesses such as newsagents tend to locate away from rivals. If they are too close together they will split the market and lose sales.

Businesses with more than one location

For some businesses, even though the head office is located in a particular area, they operate in other areas. For example, the Boots Head Office is in Nottingham but the company has stores everywhere in the UK. This means that the Boots market is national. Boots and Marks & Spencer might have more than one site or store in the same town. Marks & Spencer's Head Office is in London and the business not only expands nationally but also internationally. The business trades in over 683 locations across the UK and 30 locations abroad. Ford, ICI, IBM, Shell and Coca-Cola sell their products worldwide.

 **ACTIVITY**

Find out from the *Yellow Pages* the following:

1 a business which has more than one site in your local area.
2 a business which has different sites and location throughout the country.

Key Terms

Bulk-decreasing industry An industry which is located near the natural resources, because the raw material is bulky, for example, stainless steel in Sheffield.

Bulk-increasing industry An industry which is located near the market because the final product is bulky or fragile, for example, biscuits and garden furniture.

85

Chapter 8 How competitors affect business activities

Any business that hopes to be successful needs to be aware of the needs and wants of its customers and to work hard to satisfy and meet these needs and wants.

In a mixed economy such as the UK, where the ownership of resources is shared between the private and the public sectors, there are elements of competition. Businesses in the private sector are in constant competition to attract more customers by using a variety of methods.

BP (British Petroleum) is a very large business which operates nationally and internationally. Internationally the business's main competitors include Shell, Esso and Texaco, and at the national level, state and independent oil companies. In Europe, the company is in competition with supermarkets and hypermarkets, e.g. Tesco and Sainsbury's petrol stations, for fuel sales among customers.

ACTIVITY: TYPE OF COMPETITION

Fill in the following sentence using one of three words: **local**, **national**, **international**

I   A grocery business in Huddersfield which is owned by two partners mainly faces .... competition.

2   River Island is a private limited company which has different stores throughout the UK, and it therefore faces .... competition.

3   Marks and Spencer has stores not only in the UK but also in Europe and the USA.

Therefore it faces .... and .... competition.

Methods of competition

In order to satisfy the wants and needs of the customers the business must carefully combine the following elements: the right **Product**, at the right **Price** in the right **Place** with the right **Promotion** methods. This is known as the 4 Ps.

Businesses compete in different ways:

1   developing new products
2   improving existing products
3   changing their prices
4   developing new packaging and design
5   improving customer service and building up a new reputation.

Businesses compete by making their products look and sound different from those made by their competitors. This is called adding value to the product. Value can be added in various different ways, for example: improving the packaging and design of the product; giving the product an attractive brand name and image; displaying the product on the shelves in an exciting way; providing better customer service.

Developing new products

For a business to be successful and able to compete it needs to respond to changes in:

• customer needs and wants
• customer attitudes

- customer tastes
- the environment
- economic conditions
- the climate
- competition
- supplier attitudes
- the law
- fashion
- technology.

Improving customer service

Having sold a product to the customer, all of the departments in the business must see that the consumer is content with the product.

Changing their prices

The actual prices that a business charges for its products will depend on whether it is trying to win a massive share of the market, or whether it wants consumers to buy its product because it is different to, or better than, a rival's products. Setting the right price is important to:

- attract more customers
- compete with rival businesses (competitors)
- make a healthy profit.

ACTIVITY

1 In your group, choose 20 different products, and find out the price of each in three different supermarkets. Enter your findings in a table.
   a Add up the total prices for the 20 products for each supermarket.
   b Which supermarket is the cheapest?
   c Which supermarket is the most expensive?
   d Find out if people you know who regularly shop in these places agree with your findings.

2 Choose one of the products which is sold at different prices by different supermarkets, for example, bread.
   a Find out which firm charges the lowest price.
   b Find out which firm charges the highest price.
   c Find out which firm charges an average price.
   d Ask people you know who regularly go shopping which price they would be prepared to pay from the above range of prices for this product.

CASE STUDY — Boots and the competition

John Boot was born in Radcliffe-on-Trent in 1815 and his early life was spent as an agricultural worker on local farms. He travelled to attend services at the Wesleyan chapels in the Lace Market area of Nottingham. It was a poor area and John Boot became involved in chapel affairs and local schemes to improve living conditions within his community.

At that time, herbal remedies were

popular among poor people who could not afford the services of a physician. In 1849, with the assistance of his mother, father-in-law and the support of the local Methodist Community, John opened the British and American Botanic Establishment at 6 Goose Gate, hoping to provide comfort to the needy, as well as a reasonable living for his family. John and his wife Mary gave consultations to poor people and prepared many remedies themselves. However, in 1860, after hard work and ill health, John died at the age of 45. His wife Mary and their son Jesse took over the management of the shop.

When Jesse Boot reached the age of 21, he became a partner in the business, which then began to trade under the name of M & J Boot, Herbalists. To beat his competitors, Jesse cut his prices and asked customers to pay cash rather than take credit. He advertised extensively and began to sell an ever wider range of stock; 'over 2000 articles' as one advert claimed. In 1877 Jesse took sole control of the shop and became the largest dealer in herbal medicines and one of the busiest shopkeepers in Nottingham.

The business needed more space. With financial support from several local business contacts, Jesse took on a lease, and converted a property at 16-20 Goosegate into a shop. It contained the retail and wholesale shops, workshops, stockrooms, office and living accommodation. In 1883 the business became a private limited company.

Following the expansion of the Goosegate shop, Jesse wanted to repeat its success elsewhere in Nottingham. He bought up vacant properties across the city – often

sites in poorer areas where properties were reasonably cheap. To beat his competitors, and to promote the business further, each new shop was opened with a great deal of publicity.

The success of the business provoked a hostile reaction from many fellow chemists, who criticised the cut-price tactics and tried to cast doubt on some of Boots' products.

In 1879 the House of Lords supported the right of general stores and companies, as well as traditional chemists, to dispense medicines. Jesse therefore sought a qualified pharmacist in order to offer dispensing services. To build up public confidence in the quality and purity of his products, in 1888 Jesse renamed the business Boots Pure Drug Company.

Read the above case study carefully and answer the following questions:

1 What were the main business objectives for Boots?

2 Who were Boots' main competitors?

3 Why do you think the local community supported John Boot?

4 What was Boots' main product?

5 How did John Boot come up with the idea of developing this product?

6 When Jesse Boot took over the management of the business, one of his main aims was to beat the competition. Explain how John responded to his competitors.

7 What were the main factors which Jesse considered in choosing the location of his shops?

Key Terms

Competition The idea that in a market one producer should always be rivalled by another producer to ensure that prices are kept low and the customer is not exploited.

Competitive business Where a business is more able to compete to attract more customers.

Demand The desire or need of a consumer backed up by the ability to pay over a period of time.

Efficiency The effective use of a business's resources without waste of time or materials.

Price The market value of goods and services that are bought by consumers and firms.

Product development The process of a business bringing new products into the market or adapting and improving upon existing products.

Value added Adding value to a product to make it look more attractive for customers without adding too much to the cost.

Want The desire or need of a consumer to buy goods or services; if backed up by the ability to pay, this becomes demand.

Chapter 9 Businesses and their stakeholders

Businesses make decisions regarding their objectives, activities and location. Stakeholders are the people who can influence these decisions. You are going to learn:

* who they are
* how they can influence businesses
* how businesses react to this influence.

All organisations have a responsibility to their stakeholders. Stakeholders are individuals and groups who have a stake in the running of the organisation. Stakeholders may include shareholders, suppliers, customers, employees and managers, as well as the government and society as a whole. Stakeholders can influence business decisions in a variety of ways, such as the following.

* Customers need to be satisfied; they have a choice as to where they buy products.
* Employees can choose whether or not to work for a certain business organisation.
* Shareholders carefully select organisations in which to invest their money.
* The government can impose rules and regulations on businesses to ensure that customers are not exploited and employees are working in safe conditions.

Therefore, to satisfy stakeholders, a business needs to develop codes of conduct, stating clearly the way in which the business will carry out its activities.

Shareholders

The main role of shareholders in a business is:

* to vote or elect directors who make

decisions on their behalf
* to invest in the business, so they have a right to a share in the profits.

Shareholders will play no part in the day-to-day running or management of the organisation.

ACTIVITY

Discuss in your groups the following sentence.

'Shareholders exercise influence on businesses to increase and maximise the profits.'

The Government

The government can impose rules and regulations on business activities to ensure that:

* business activities are legal
* business activities are safe and do not harm the community
* customers are not exploited
* the product which a business sells is safe
* employees are protected in the workplace
* business activities do not harm the environment.

Employees

Employees are the workforce which is employed by a business. Employees could be either the management team, supervisors, or the rest of the workforce.

Employers could be sole traders, partners in a partnership or a limited company.

With the extension of education and improvements in living standards,

The employees of a bike shop are stakeholder's in the business's activities

employees demand more than financial rewards. As people spend a large part of their life at work, it is important that they get some satisfaction from their jobs.

Not all jobs can give satisfaction, and people have different ideas of what constitutes a good job. For some people pay is the most important factor, while others will have some other priority. Often it is a combination of many factors which makes a job satisfying.

The following are just some of these factors:

- pay and opportunity for wage increases
- promotion prospects
- working hours and times of attendance
- holiday arrangements
- conditions in which work is carried out
- style of management
- communication in the workplace
- training.

Management

Managers are employees in the business who act on behalf of shareholders (who elected them), and their main role is to protect shareholders' interests.

CASE STUDY – Business Council planning action

The staff and workforce at Harwood PLC have created a joint council to discuss industrial action. The move at one of the companies in West Yorkshire is a direct result of a pay offer they labelled "miserly". One of their first tasks will be to co-ordinate industrial action at the company next week.

Ms Janet Ayton, the trade union representative in the company and chairman of the new group, said 'This is the second year that staff had been offered a pay rise below inflation. Over the same two years the Managing Director has seen his pay rise by a staggering 47%.'

The workforce in the company are among the lowest paid in the country and all are seriously overworked.

Read the case study carefully and answer the following questions:

1 What is the workforce at Harwood PLC angry about?

2 What sort of action are the workforce threatening to take?

3 How does the workforce in Harwood PLC exercise pressure on management?

Customers

A successful business is a business which identifies customer needs and wants and works hard to satisfy these needs and wants. Therefore, customers exercise constant pressures on businesses to make them develop, and supply, the right **Product** at the right **Price** in the right **Place**.

ACTIVITY: CUSTOMERS AND PRESSURES

Customers are very important stakeholders who influence businesses. In this activity you are going to learn how businesses should respond to customer pressures.

Using your business knowledge and the information above, try to complete the following statements with the words in the box.

Customers can influence businesses to:

1 .... existing products.

2 .... new products.

3 .... that they need and want.

4 .... to changes in lifestyle.

| develop |
| respond |
| provide |
| improve |

Competitors

Businesses are in constant competition to satisfy customer needs and wants. Competitors influence business decisions in one way or another. For a business to survive in the market it must be able to compete by offering lower prices, better quality products, or produce new products.

ACTIVITY: THE ROLE OF COMPETITORS

Using your business knowledge, complete the following statements with the words in the box.

Competitors influence businesses to:

1 .... their prices.

2 .... the quality of their products.

3 .... new products.

4 .... new technology.

| reduce |
| improve |
| provide |
| develop |

 ACTIVITY

In your groups, think of two or three businesses which are in the same area of production, for example, supermarkets, car manufacturers, hairdressers, etc. Discuss how these businesses compete with each other and who benefits from this competition.

Local community and its concerns for the environment

The local community can be a very important external influence on business decisions. For example, the local community might protest against the building of a new supermarket, a pub or an industrial estate in the local area. Businesses are also aware that their customers are the local community. Therefore, one of the prime aims of any business is to gain local community support for their activities.

Promoting businesses' image in the local community

Most businesses seek to establish good relations with the local community through such activities such as sponsoring schools' computers, raising money for charitable events, and participating in school and college activities.

Inviting employers to participate in group activities at school or college doesn't only strengthen the links with local firms but also:

1 enables you to engage actively with new subject matter
2 challenges and encourages you to participate in practical activities
3 adds a touch of reality to group activities
4 promotes your communication and presentation skills
5 adds more fun to the learning environment, as students usually like to see and work with different people
6 allows you to explore opportunities for short-term work placement
7 enhances your confidence in working with strangers.

 ## ACTIVITIES

1 Look in your local newspaper for an example of a pressure group in your local area; for example, local residents protest at the building of a new road, supermarket or an industrial estate near where they live. Express your views on the problem.
2 In your groups describe briefly an event in your school or college where employers from local firms were invited to take part. Try to evaluate their contribution to the event and to the school or college.

CASE STUDY –
Battle win for noise row hotel

A hotel owner has won his battle for a new entertainment licence after a row with local residents over noise.

Mr Robert Grey, the owner of Come Inn Hotel, says he is doing all he can to reduce noise and has employed a noise consultant in a bid to end complaints. Mr Grey's entertainment licence has been renewed by Calderdale Council Licensing sub-committee, despite objections from local residents. Six people wrote letters asking councillors to pull the plug on the permit because of loud music, late night parties, rowdiness and door slamming.

Some residents from the recently built development near the hotel said the situation was making their lives a misery.

Mr Grey who has owned the premises for 15 years said he was also working closely with the council's environmental department and the noise has always been monitored.

Mr Grey said he had received no complaints before the development was built last year.

Read the above case study carefully and answer the following:

- What did the local residents complain about?
- Why do the local residents put pressure on Mr Grey's business?
- How might this pressure affect Mr Grey's business?
- Why did the local council permit Mr Grey to continue his business?

Other examples of businesses' involvement with the local community

CASE STUDY — McDonald's and the environment

McDonald's is very aware that the local communities in which it operates are an important stakeholder in its business activities. Because many of these communities are concerned with the environmental issues, McDonald's is keen to let them know about its commitment to helping the environment. McDonald's produces literature about its policies on subjects such as diet and the preservation of the rain forests and also sponsors a number of environmental initiatives, many in local communities. Examples of McDonald's environmental work include the following.

Conservation

McDonald's does not purchase beef whose production threatens tropical rain forests anywhere in the world. It does not use any South American or Central American beef for hamburgers sold in the USA or Canada. Only 100% pure USDA-inspected domestic US beef is used. McDonald's also monitors suppliers' plants and checks government stamps to make sure that suppliers do not sell any beef that has been imported from another area.

Litter control

Since 1988, McDonald's, in partnership with the Tidy Britain group, has sponsored the 'Bin it for Britain' and 'National Spring Clean' campaigns. 'Bin it for Britain' is designed to encourage good litter behaviour in young people. Every day McDonald's staff regularly collect all rubbish (not only

McDonald's packaging) dropped in the vicinity of the restaurant.

Many of McDonald's restaurants organise their litter-related competitions with local schools, colleges and youth groups.

Recycling

McDonald's, in line with its stated policy of fostering quality environmental practices, helped to promote recycling of aluminium cans in Staffordshire by working with the local authority, community groups, schools, colleges and the Aluminium Can Recycling Association (ACRA).

Built environment

McDonald's takes a sensitive approach to its built environment, working closely with planning and conservation officers to preserve buildings of architectual merit and to improve the townscape.

McDonald's has successfully integrated into many listed buildings and conservation areas including restaurants in Windsor, Cambridge, York and Shrewsbury as well as Tower Hill and Fleet Street in London.

In many towns McDonald's has invested considerable sums in restoring old buildings, often putting back architectural details that have been lost. York, Chester and Stratford-upon-Avon are prime examples.

After reading this case study with your tutor, answer the following questions:

1 Many of McDonald's restaurants organise their litter-related competitions with local schools, colleges and youth groups. Visit McDonald's restaurant(s) in your local area and find out if any are or have been involved in litter-related competitions with local schools and colleges.

2 Find out if your school or college has been involved in any of the litter-related competitions with McDonald's or other businesses.

3 Find out examples of other businesses which support the environment.

Stakeholders and conflict of interests

It is obvious that stakeholders have different interests and see business success in different ways. The criteria for success vary from one group to another, depending on their interests and the role they play to influence the business.

CASE STUDY — The Body Shop approach to stakeholders

In 1976, Anita Roddick opened the first Body Shop in Brighton, selling 25 naturally based skin and hair care products. The Body Shop International PLC has over 1500 shops in 47 countries selling more than 400 different products. The Body Shop, however, is not just a highly successful manufacturer and retailer of toiletries and cosmetics. The whole organisation is committed to issues such as respect for human rights, animal and environmental protection.

Although the business's main objective is to maximise profit and look after the environment, The Body Shop recognises that there are a number of different groups in society with an interest in its performance. These groups, or stakeholders, may have different priorities. The way the business operates affects them, and their interests may influence the way the business sets its objectives and how it seeks to achieve them.

The management team of The Body Shop must run the business in such a way as to satisfy the different groups of stakeholders. This may not be easy and conflicts of interest may develop.

1 Employees

The Body Shop directly employs 2500 staff at the headquarters in Littlehampton and all company-owned facilities and shops in the UK. Fair income, promotion and training opportunities are methods of motivating employees to work hard.

Workers' rights include a safe, healthy working atmosphere, fair wage rate and no discrimination on the grounds of race, gender, or sexual orientation.

2 Customers

In the 52 weeks to 28 February 1997, The Body Shop recorded 87 million customer transactions. This means that every 0.4 seconds, someone, somewhere buys something from The Body Shop. Customer care therefore has become a crucial part of the trading policy. The Body Shop customers demand not only high quality, value-for-money products, but also recognise the need for environmental responsibility. The customer needs to be well informed in order to make responsible choices.

3 Suppliers

The Body Shop has hundreds of suppliers, all of whom have their own stakeholders to satisfy. For smaller suppliers, profit and income may be significant, but also discounts and payment periods may be important.

4 Community Trade suppliers

This is a group of 25 suppliers in 13 countries (as at May 1997), such as Brazil, Ghana and Bangladesh, specifically chosen because they are struggling economically. The Body Shop believes that this trade should be more than the simple exchange of goods and currency (money). It wants to help create livelihoods and support development in those countries. The Body Shop offers its knowledge and training in exchange for materials from these countries. These communities clearly have a stake in the future success of the organisation.

5 Shareholders

The Body Shop is a public limited company and its shareholders are the legal owners. Although the shareholders recognise the company's social and economic commitments, the share price remains important. A falling share price can wipe millions of pounds off the value of a company. In theory, if the shareholders are dissatisfied with the performance of the company, they can remove the Board of Directors at the Annual General Meeting.

6 Local community

Although The Body Shop has many objectives, it is part of a local community and, therefore, has a responsibility to the community in which it operates and the local economy. For example, in a town with unemployment above the national average, The Body Shop is the second largest employer. Job creation is therefore very important to the town. The Body Shop also allows its employees paid time off to do voluntary work in their local community.

With your tutor, read the above case study carefully and answer the following question:

The above case shows that The Body Shop has several stakeholders who have an interest in the business. In this task you are going to match the following statements (the interests of a stakeholder) with the right stakeholder.

Statements

1 'I want to be heard, I have questions I need answering. I ensure that my voice matters.'

2 'So you don't test your products or ingredients on animals, but how do I know your suppliers are not doing it?'

3 'I want to know what I have in common with other suppliers to The Body Shop. I want to share my experience and learn how we can improve together.'

4 'What I want is a livelihood that will last. So that my daughters can live a life that is better than mine.'

5 'How do I balance concern for human rights with my financial return?'

6 'Everybody is trying to tell us about the community – politicians, business people, everybody. Instead of telling us, why don't they include us? Don't we all belong?'

Stakeholders:

a local community

b customers

c shareholders

d suppliers

e employees

f community trade suppliers.

Unit 2 Test your knowledge

This is a quick test to help you check how much you have understood.

In the following statements, there are some right and some wrong answers. Circle only the **wrong** answer/answers.

1   In a sole trader business:

    a   the owner has limited liability
    b   the owner runs the business
    c   the owner can employ other people to work for him
    d   the owner takes all the profit.

2   The scale of a business refers to:

    a   the type of market the product is sold in
    b   the size of business
    c   the location of the business.

3   In the UK the private sector:

    a   is owned by the government
    b   is owned by private individuals
    c   is controlled by private enterprises.

4   The public sector in the UK mainly exists:

    a   to provide services to the local and national community
    b   to compete with the private sector
    c   to make profit.

5   A public limited company is:

    a   owned by the public
    b   in the public sector
    c   in the private sector.

6   For a private limited company:

    a   business affairs are public
    b   business is privately owned by family and friends

    c   the ownership is in the private sector.

7   A bulk-decreasing industry is an industry which:

    a   is located near the raw materials
    b   is located near the market
    c   could be located anywhere
    d   involves a low transport cost for the final product.

8   A business scale could be measured by:

    a   the number of its employees
    b   the number of business sites
    c   the size of the market share
    d   the amount of capital invested.

9   The primary sector is concerned with:

    a   the extraction of raw materials from the ground
    b   the manufacturing of raw materials
    c   the distribution of raw materials
    d   the distribution of the final product.

10 Banks and building societies are:

    a   in the secondary sector
    b   in the primary sector
    c   in the tertiary sector.

11 Toyota car manufacturer mainly operates in:

    a   the primary sector
    b   the secondary sector
    c   the tertiary sector.

12 Dobsons & Sons Ltd is an example of:

    a   a private limited company
    b   a public limited company
    c   a public corporation.

13 A public corporation, for example, the BBC is:

a in the primary sector
b in the public sector
c owned by the government.

14 Declining industries, for example, mining and fishing, mainly exist in:

a the secondary sector
b the primary sector
c the private sector
d the tertiary sector.

15 In a sole trader business the number of owners are:

a 1–5
b only 1
c more than 5.

16 A sole trader business is a small business because:

a there is only one owner
b it is in the private sector
c the site of the business is usually small.

17 In a partnership business, partners might draw up a legal agreement which is called:

a a job contract
b a contract of employment
c a deed of partnership.

18 In a partnership, partners usually have:

a limited liability
b unlimited liability
c active role in the running of the business.

19 In the public sector the entrepreneur (owner of resources) is:

a the government
b public
c The board of directors.

20 Customers are the group of people who:

a run a business
b own a business
c buy a product.

Unit 2 Assessment

Check with your tutor what you need to produce for your portfolio. If you do the assignment below, you will be on your way to completing the work you will need to do.

1   Choose two businesses to find out about. Make sure that you pick two different kinds of business. For example, one could be a business that provides a service while the other could produce goods. Or, one of the business could be a large, well-known company, while the other could be a small family business.

2   Find out the following information about each business.

 a How is the business owned, e.g., is it a sole trader, a partnership, or a PLC? What are the main features of this type of ownership? Why is this type of ownership suited to the business? Can you say how another form of ownership would make the business different?

 b What does the business do? Describe its main activities. How does it carry out these activities?

 c Where is the business located? What are the reasons for its location, e.g., how easy is it to get to?

 d Who are the business's main competitors? What do these competitor businesses do and where are they located?

 e Who are the business's main stakeholders? Describe them. Why is the business important to these people? Who do you think are the business's most important stakeholders?

3   Use your word processing skills to write a report about everything you have found out about each of your two chosen businesses. Base the report on your answers to question 2. As well as describing each business's ownership, location and stakeholders, try to write about how things like the business's location and stakeholders affect what happens to the business and how it is run.

UNIT 2 ASSESSMENT

All businesses need accurate financial information in order to succeed. This can be achieved only by effective communication and organisation between different departments.

When businesses communicate with other businesses or customers, they will need to use financial documents. Businesses use some of these documents when they make purchases from suppliers, others when they sell products to customers.

It is very important for a business to record its financial transactions in the most effective way. In this unit you are going to learn about:

- business costs and revenues
- how to work out a business profit
- financial documents and what they are for
- how financial documents are used
- how payments are made
- methods of making and receiving payments.

Chapter 10 Investigating cost and revenue, profit and loss

Money is an important resource for a firm. Without it, the firm will be unable to pay its workers, buy raw materials or purchase machinery. Money flows through the organisation as it is received from customers and is passed on to workers or suppliers.

A successful business will need to control both the inflow and the outflow of money. In large firms this will be done by a finance department headed by qualified accountants. The job of the finance department is to keep records of payments and receipts and to make information available to help in decision making.

capital money machinery buildings

Flow of money

Somebody provides the money to start up the business in the first place. Extra finance may have to be introduced into the business if it is to develop and expand.

Where does the money come from?

* The owners of the business can provide funds themselves from their own savings.
* Money or funds can be provided from profits which are not taken out of the firm but used instead to buy more resources.
* There are also a number of possible sources of finance available to a firm from people outside the organisation, for example, arranging loans from banks.

Money is used to pay for the following:

* raw materials
* wages
* replacement of old equipment

Many owners get the money to start a business by arranging a bank loan

* dividends (share of profits to shareholders)
* taxes
* retained profits for future investment.

Because firms will often have to pay for labour and raw materials before they sell their goods or services, there is always a risk that the money coming into the firm (revenue) will be less than the money that is being paid out (costs). Those people providing finance (e.g. banks) will therefore want a reward for taking the risk of not being repaid.

What is the reward?

Profit is the reward that goes to the owner of the business if it succeeds.

Interest is the reward that is paid to the lender (for example, a bank) for lending the money to the business.

ACTIVITY: BUSINESS REVENUE AND COSTS

Sort out the information below into the following two groups:

1 business revenue
2 business costs.

Cash   Rent   Wages   Cost of raw materials   Advertising expenses   Interest on loans   Insurance premium   Transport expenses   Payment for market research   Income from ice cream sales   Heating   Electricity   Income from selling   Insurance policies   Petrol

Factors which affect a business's sales income and costs (spending)

Revenue and spending vary from one business to another. It depends on many factors such as:

* size of business
* what the business sells, e.g. goods or services
* the number of employees in the business
* the number of business premises
* the number of products which a business sells
* the price of the product.

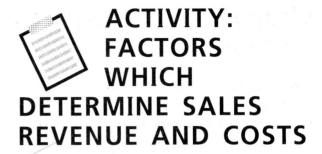

ACTIVITY: FACTORS WHICH DETERMINE SALES REVENUE AND COSTS

Fill in the following statements using one of two words, **costs** or **revenue** (sometimes you can use both words):

1 The bigger the business size the higher the .... and the ....
2 The more employees a business has the higher the ....
3 The more a business sells the more .... it receives.
4 The more premises a business has the higher the ....

Profit

Profit is the money left from sales revenue after taking away all costs.

Profit = Revenue − Costs

Working out costs and revenue

Most, if not all, businesses in the private sector work for profit, whether they are selling goods or providing services. Each business should be able to work out its:

1 costs
2 income
3 profits/losses.

For a business to make profit, it needs to generate income that is greater than its costs.

Types of costs

There are two different types of costs that a business has to estimate and then work out accurately.

1 Start-up costs (non-trading expenses)

These are costs that a business pays on any non-trading expense, i.e. paying for market research, buying premises and capital items such as machinery or computer equipment which must be bought before the business can start trading.

2 Running costs (trading expenses)

These are the expenses that relate to business trading activities, including VAT (Value Added Tax). Examples of trading expenses are:

- cost of raw materials
- salaries and wages
- rent
- council tax
- bills
- VAT
- petty cash.

Types of running costs – fixed or variable?
Fixed costs are costs that do not change from one month to the next, no matter how many goods or items the business produces or how many clients to which it provides its services. For example, the cost of renting, heating and insuring premises for a hairdressing business will not be affected by the number of customers whose hair is blow-dried or trimmed.

Variable costs do change from one month to the next, depending upon the quantity of goods or items produced by the company or the number of clients to which it provides a service. For example, in a hairdressing salon, the cost of shampoo, conditioner and styling products will depend on how many customers are seen.

Do your calculations in stages
Stage 1: Fixed costs or overheads
These are costs that have to be met regardless of whether a business sells its product or service. When the Light Delight Ice Cream business was set up, Liz and Margaret needed to think about the following:

1 the cost of hiring or renting a place to work from

2 the cost of running this place, e.g. heating, water rate, electricity etc.

3 the cost of employing people to work for them.

Margaret and Liz were aware that they would have to pay the above costs regardless of the amount of ice cream they produced and sold every day.

Stage 2: Variable or direct costs
When Margaret and Liz set up the Light Delight Ice Cream business, they knew that there were other costs that they had to pay on top of the monthly fixed costs. They needed to buy raw materials to make the ice cream, for example, sugar, fruit, cream, etc. These costs change depending on the amount of ice cream they make. The more ice cream they produce, the more raw materials they need to buy. These costs are called variable costs.

Stage 3: Total running costs
You can now work out exactly what costs a business such as Light Delight would face:

Total running cost = fixed costs + variable costs

ACTIVITY

Steve Howe, the owner of Pine Tree Furniture, realised that the business total cost (fixed + variable) was too high.

1 Suggest two ways for a business to reduce its costs.

2 Which way is more practical and under the control of the business? Explain your answer.

Business income (revenue)

Income or revenue is the money a business makes from selling its products or seervices. For example, if Pine Tree Furniture sells 100 tables at £10 a table, the total sales income will be £1000. Therefore, to work out business income or revenue, we need to work out:

- the price per item or unit (this could be for a product or a service)
- the number of items or units a business sells.

ACTIVITY

Sarah Woodhead is a hairdresser who works from home. Work out her total revenue in January if she has 10 regular customers, 4 of whom have their hair cut and blow-dried and 6 of whom have their hair coloured. She charges £8 for a cut and blow dry and £15 for colouring.

32 +90   £ 122

Working out the price

Every business needs to decide on a reasonable price to charge its customers.

Here they will have to use some business judgement:

- If they charge more than their competitors, they may not sell anything.
- If they charge too little, they may not cover their costs.

The owner or the management of a business must make sure that whatever they suggest is a reasonable price. It should be enough to cover the variable costs plus enough to make a contribution towards paying their fixed costs.

> Revenue = Number of sold items × Price

ACTIVITY

1 From the above information fill in the gaps in the following sentences using only one of two words, **higher** or **lower**.

The .... the number of sold items, the .... the price the more the business income.

The .... the number of sold items, the .... the price the less the business income.

2 From the above information suggest two ways to increase Pine Tree Furniture's income (revenue).

Working out a business profit or a loss

In its simplest terms, a business profit could be worked out from the formula below:

> Profit = Income (Revenue) − Total
> running costs

Remember: to calculate a business profit, you have to consider the total running costs (fixed and variable), and the total revenue. A business makes profit if the total revenue covers the running costs. The cost of machines and equipment (start-up cost) is not added to the total cost.

In the first few years of a business's life, it might make enough income to cover its running costs. Even so, the start-up cost is not yet covered.

ACTIVITY

Fill in the gaps in the following sentences using one of the words **bigger** or **smaller**.

1 A business will make profit if its income is ...b...... than its costs.
2 A business will make losses if its costs are ....b... than its income.
3 A business will make profit if its costs are ...s.... than its income.
4 A business will make losses if its income is ....s.... than its costs.

ACTIVITY

1 If a business makes losses, from the information above suggest two ways to reduce its losses and perhaps to change them into profits.

2 What happens if a business income equals its costs?

ACTIVITY

1 Will the business make a profit if its total income equals total revenue? no
     cost
2 Will the business make a loss if its total income equals total revenue? no
     cost

ACTIVITY

Delicious Bakery is a business that was set up in January 1997. Peter Davies, the owner, invested £10,000 to buy new equipment and computers for the business. During the year, Peter had to pay for the following items:

Wages	£5,500
Heating	£1,500
Electricity	£750
Leaflets	£500
Advertisement in the local newspaper	£250
Insurance	£500
Transport	£650
Rent	£3,500
Council tax	£750

Peter also had to pay £3,500 for flour, sugar, milk and other ingredients to make bread, cakes, muffins, sandwiches and buns.

At the end of the year the business made £15,500 revenue from selling bread, sandwiches, cakes, muffins and buns.

1 Work out:
   a the total start-up cost for Delicious Bakery £10000
   b the business's total fixed costs in 1997 £10400
   c the business's total variable costs in 1997
   d the business's total running costs in 1997
   e the business's losses or profit at the end of the year L = £8400

2 Peter had to pay the following costs during the year 1998:

Wages	£5,500
Heating	£1,500
Electricity	£750
Insurance	£500
Transport	£650
Rent	£3,500
Council tax	£750

Peter also had to pay £4,500 for flour, sugar, milk and other ingredients to make bread, cakes, muffins, sandwiches and buns.

At the end of the year the business made £20,500 in revenue from selling bread, sandwiches, cakes, muffins and buns.

a What is the business's start-up cost? *0*

b What is the business's total fixed costs? *10250*

c What is the business's total variable *7400* costs?

d What is the business's total running costs? *17650*

e Compare the business's running costs for 1998 with the running costs for 1997. Why do you think this is the case? *made more breads in 1997*

f What happened to the business's sales revenue in 1998? Why do you think this is the case? *began popular*

g What is the business's loss or profit at the end of 1998? *+ 2850*

ACTIVITY

The Pine Tree Furniture business manages to reduce its monthly fixed costs to £1,000, and the selling price per table is to be £55. The business sells 100 tables. The cost of wood to make each table is £50.

1 Work out the business's total income. *55×100 5500*

2 Work out the business's total variable costs. *5000*

3 Work out the business's total running costs. *6000*

4 Work out the business's losses or profits. *c 500*

5 If the business does not make a profit, suggest two ways for the business to make enough income/revenue to cover (equal) its total cost. *cheaper raw materials.*

ACTIVITY: WORKING OUT A BUSINESS'S TOTAL COSTS AND INCOME

This activity helps you to learn and understand:

* the meaning of fixed costs
* the meaning of variable costs
* the meaning of income (revenue)
* reasons for a business being unable to generate income.

Output	Fixed costs	Variable costs	Total costs	Revenue	Profit/ Loss
0	1000	0	1000	0	(1000)
1	1000	500	1500	700	(800)
2	1000	1000	2000	1400	(600)
3	1000	1500	2500	2100	(400)
4	1000	2000	3000	2800	(200)
5	1000	2500	3500	3500	0 —Break-even
6	1000	3000	4000	4200	200
7	1000	3500	4500	4900	400

* The business's monthly fixed costs = £1000.
* The cost of raw materials (wood) per table = £500.
* Total costs = Fixed costs + Variable costs.
* The selling price for each table is £700.

Formulas to remember:

a Variable costs = Price of raw material per unit × No. of units

b Revenue = Selling price per unit × No. of units.

Look carefully at the table above and tick the correct statement at each level of production:

At level 0 of output:
1 Total costs are less than Revenue.
② Total costs are more than Revenue.
3 Total costs equal Revenue.

At level 1 of output:
1 Total costs are less than Revenue.
② Total costs are more than Revenue.
3 Total costs equal Revenue.

At level 2 of output:
1 Total costs are less than Revenue.
② Total costs are more than Revenue.
3 Total costs equal Revenue.

At level 3 of output:
1 Total costs are less than Revenue.
② Total costs are more than Revenue.
3 Total costs equal Revenue.

At level 4 of output:
1 Total costs are less than Revenue.
② Total costs are more than Revenue.
3 Total costs equal Revenue.

At level 5 of output:
1 Total costs are less than Revenue.
2 Total costs are more than Revenue.
③ Total costs equal Revenue.

At level 6 of output:
① Total costs are less than Revenue.
2 Total costs are more than Revenue.
3 Total costs equal Revenue.

Key Terms

Competition The idea that in a market one business should always be rivalled by another business to ensure that prices are kept low and the customer is not exploited.

Consumer A person who buys goods and services for his or her own use or consumption.

Costs The money a business spends in order to produce goods and services for its customers.

Fixed costs or overheads Those costs of a business that remain unchanged whatever the level of output the business is producing over a period of time.

Profit What is left when all costs incurred in making and selling a product are deducted from the revenue gained from that sale.

Risk All business decisions involve an element of risk because there are a number of possible outcomes from a decision. For example, there is a risk in setting up a business because it might fail. Owners are rewarded with profit for taking this risk and investing their money in the business.

Running costs These are the expenses that relate to business trading activities, including VAT.

Sales revenue The income that a business receives as a result of selling its products.

Sales revenue = Price × Quantity sold

Start-up costs These are costs that a business pays on any non-trading expenses, i.e. capital items such as machinery or computer equipment.

Turnover The value of sales over a period of time (sales revenue). Total sales.

Variable costs Those costs that change directly with the output of a business, i.e. raw material cost, overtime cost, fuel and power cost.

At level 7 of output:
1 Total costs are less than Revenue.
2 Total costs are more than Revenue.
3 Total costs equal Revenue.

From your findings answer the following questions:

1 At which levels of production (output) are there profits? *6, 7*.

2 At which levels of production (output) are there losses? *0, 1, 2, 3, 4*.

3 At which level of production is there is no loss and no profit? Why do think this is the case? *5. same total costs and revenue*

Book keeping

You have learnt a simple way to work out a business's losses and profit. In reality it is more complex than that. This is because other factors need to be considered, for example:

1 Business revenue from selling products is not the only source of revenue. There are other sources, for example, interest received on savings or investment.

2 Businesses, when working out whether they have made a profit or a loss, need to consider the start-up costs. Start-up costs are costs that need to be met before the business can start trading, for example, the cost of market research and buying machines and equipment.

3 Not all sales revenue arrives in cash. Businesses sometimes sell products to customers on credit.

4 The above simple analysis does not show the change in sales revenue and cost from one month to another.

5 The above simple analysis does not show the period of time, for example, a week or a month, when these revenues and costs were made.

Why keep accounts?

Businesses need to keep track and record their financial transactions. This is the most basic part of any system of accounts. It is a record of all payments by the business and the money it receives. Small businesses can buy books already set out for this purpose.

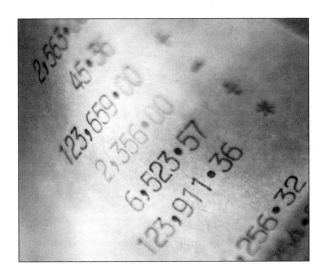

What financial information must be kept?

All businesses must keep records of their sales revenue and the costs that they have paid to make and sell their products. To do this all businesses should do the following:

1 keep all invoices raised on behalf of the business

2 keep all sales invoices numbered sequentially

3 keep all purchase invoices received and listed

4 record all wages and salaries paid

5 keep all cheque-book stubs, paying-in slips/books and business bank account statements

6 keep a full record of VAT, whether paid by or to the business.

Business budget

Businesses need to plan and estimate their income and costs. This plan is called a budget. It is a statement of the estimated income and expenditure (spending) of a business over a particular period of time, usually one year. A budget enables the business to:

1 work out the total business expenditure and income

2 find out if there are any liquidity problems (if a business's cash income is less than its cash expenditure)

3 show how the business managed to cover its shortage of cash, e.g. arranged for a short-term loan or an overdraft.

ACTIVITY: SETTING UP A SPREADSHEET FOR A BUSINESS BUDGET

Setting up a spreadsheet for a business budget

Below is the cash budget for Trading Ltd.

a Set up a spreadsheet with 13 columns and 12 rows.

b In the spreadsheet, enter the text for each column and row heading, as shown below.

c Enter the figures shown below for the months January to December.

d Using the spreadsheet, calculate the totals for the column so you have the total monthly costs (expenditure) for all the items, such as purchases, wages, rent, etc.

Item	Jan	Feb	March	April	May	June	July	August	Sept	Oct	Nov	Dec
Sales	0	5,000	6,000	5,000	8,000	9,000	10,000	9,000	7,000	7,000	5,000	8,000
Grant	2,000	0,000	0,000	0,000	2,000	0,000	0,000					
Owner's capital	10,000	0,000	0,000	0,000	0,000	0,000	0,000					
TOTAL REVENUE	12000	5000	6000	5000	10000	9000	10000	9000	7000	7000	5000	8000
Purchases	5,000	3,000	5,000	6,000	4,000	3,000	4,000	4,500	3,500	3,500	3,000	5,000
Wages	1,000	1,000	1,000	2,000	2,000	2,000	2,000	2,000	1,000	1,000	1,000	2,000
Rent	500	500	500	500	500	500	500	500	500	500	500	500
Electricity	0	600	0	0	650	0	0	500	0	0	0	750
Petrol	100	150	200	150	250	250	250	200	150	150	100	200
TOTAL COSTS/ SPENDING	6600	5250	6700	8650	7400	5750	6750	7200	5150	5150	4600	8450
PROFIT/ LOSS	+5400	-250	-700	-3650	+2600	+3250	+3250	+1800	+1850	+1850	+400	-450

+3850

e Calculate the total costs (expenditure) for the year. *77650*

2 a Work out the profit and loss at the end of each month.

b Work out the profit and loss at the end of the year. *profit 15350*

Key Terms

Accounts The financial records of a business that are used by managers, owners, employees, creditors and others to show how well the business is doing.

Budget A plan showing the expected sales revenue over the coming month or year, matched against the estimated costs that will be incurred.

Cash The most liquid of all the assets that a business has. Businesses need cash to pay for the day-to-day running of the business, e.g. to pay wages, bills and for raw materials from suppliers.

Cash flow The flow of money into and out of a business.

Cashbook It is a book that is used to record the sources of income and recipients of money paid out.

Drawings The amount of money withdrawn from the business (sole trader or a partnership) for personal use.

Overdraft More cash allowed by a bank to a business or personal customer, by permitting the withdrawal of more from a current account than is in it, up to a certain limit.

Chapter II Investigating financial documents for buying and selling

Buying and selling are at the heart of business and it is very important that all sales and purchases are recorded accurately [correctly]. A customer may have been very impressed with the layout of the shop, the goods on display and any help or advice that they may have received from the sales staff. The customer may have spent some time in the shop and have been very satisfied with the goods that they have chosen. But this favourable impression of the shop will soon be destroyed if there is then a long delay or a problem of some kind at the check-out.

Therefore, the way a business handles and organises its financial documents is very important for the following reasons:

1 to provide permanent and secure [safe] records

2 to provide accounts for tax purposes

3 to provide records for transactions with customers

4 to provide records for transactions with suppliers

5 to provide records for the inflow of money

6 to provide records for the outflow of money

7 to provide records for profits and losses

There are many financial documents that any business would use to control:

• the movement of goods or services and cash out of the business

• the movement of goods or services and cash into the business.

ACTIVITY: IN OR OUT?

This activity should help you to understand the movement of transactions in and out of a business.

Fill in the gaps in the following sentences using only **out of** or **into**.

1 Goods and services move _out of_ the business when they are sold to customers.

2 Goods and services move _into_ the business when they are bought from suppliers (wholesaler or a manufacturer).

3 Cash moves _out of_ a business to pay for wages, fuel, rent, equipment and raw materials.

4 Cash moves _into_ a business to pay for sold products.

5 When goods and services get _out of_ a business, this could mean cash getting _into_ the business.

6 When cash gets _out of_ a business, this will pay for the cost of producing the products, e.g. wages, electricity, rent, raw materials, etc.

You are going to learn all about the following documents:

car
cash
Credit card

- Purchase orders
- Delivery notes
- Invoices
- Credit notes
- Statements of account sent by the business
- Remittance advice slips
- Cheques
- Receipts
- Petty cash vouchers.

A business like Light Delight Ice-cream Ltd, the fictional business you learnt about in Unit 1, would use these documents every day.

Light Delight **sends** financial documents such as delivery notes and invoices when it sells ice-cream to customers.

Light Delight **receives** financial documents such as delivery notes and invoices when it buys the materials to make ice-cream from its suppliers.

We will look at what happens at Light Delight to find out how these documents are used and to practise filling them in.

Light Delight as a supplier

The following process would take place if Sava Stores – one of Light Delight's main customers – wants to buy some Light Delight ice-cream:

a Sava Stores makes an enquiry about the price of the different flavours of ice-cream. Light Delight sends them a **price list**.

b Sava Stores makes an order by filling in an **order form**.

c Light Delight receives the order and lets the customer know that it has been received.

d Light Delight delivers the order to Sava Stores.

e Sava Stores also receives a **delivery note** from Light Delight to say that the ice-cream has been delivered.

f Sava Stores receives an **invoice** from Light Delight, asking them to pay for the ice-cream.

g Sava Stores makes their payment for the ice-cream either by **cash**, **cheque** or a **credit** or **debit card**.

h Once Light Delight receives the payment, they issue a **receipt** which says that payment has been received and send it to Sava Stores.

Light Delight as a customer

On the other hand, this is what happens when Light Delight wants to buy some items or goods from a supplier. North Dairy Milk Products Ltd is one of Light Delight's main suppliers. It supplies the business with fresh and powder milk. If Light Delight decides to order milk, they would have to go through the following process:

a Light Delight makes an enquiry about the price of the full fat, semi-skimmed and skimmed milk. They receive a **price list**.

b Light Delight makes an order by filling in an **order form**.

c North Dairy Milk Products receives the order and lets Light Delight know that it has been received.

d North Dairy Milk Products delivers the order to Light Delight.

e Light Delight also receives a **delivery note** from the supplier to say that the milk has been delivered.

f Light Delight receives an **invoice** from North Dairy Milk Products asking them to pay for the milk they have purchased.

g Light Delight pays for the milk either by **cash**, **cheque** or a **credit** or **debit card**.

h Once the payment is received by North Dairy Milk Products, they issue a receipt and send it to Light Delight saying that payment has been received

First of all, it is important to learn about the order in which these documents are usually used.

Now you are going to learn about each of the above financial documents and how to fill them in.

Catalogues or price lists

Before making an order to buy ice-cream, Sava Stores would ask for a catalogue or a price list from Light Delight. In response to a telephone call or letter of enquiry Light Delight may send a catalogue showing the full range of ice cream offered for sale and how much they charge. A price list usually shows current prices and recent

amendments, and should be referred to before placing an order.

The order (purchase order form)

To make an order, Sava Stores sends Light Delight an order form, which lists all the details of the range, flavour and prices of the ice-cream they want to buy.

Like many other businesses, Sava Stores has many checks and controls to ensure that only 'authorised' people can make orders. Many businesses use pre-printed order forms, on which there is usually a reference number. This reference number is included so that, when the goods and demand for payment are received, they can easily be checked against the original document.

LIGHT DELIGHT ICE-CREAM LTD

Unit 28 Penraven Industrial Estate
Mean Wood Road
LEEDS
LS7 2AP

Selected Price List

Ice-cream

Qty.	Item	Catalogue no.	Price
Large box	Vanilla ice-cream	CL/234	£3.25
Large box	Strawberry ice-cream	CL/235	£4.10
Large box	Chocolate ice-cream with nuts	CL/236	£5.10
Large box	Chocolate ice-cream without nuts	CL/237	£4.20
Large box	Banana ice-cream with nuts	CL/238	£5.45
Large box	Banana ice-cream without nuts	CL/239	£4.75
Large box	Raspberry ice-cream	CL/240	£4.10

Sava Stores

22 Thorncliffe Street
Fixby
Huddersfield
HD1 1GH

Order Form

From: Paul Corp
Address: As above
Order Number: ERG 6554

To: Light Delight Ice-Cream Ltd
Unit 28 Penraven Industrial Estate
Mean Wood
Leeds
LS7 2AP

VAT Reg No: 2334
Date: 26/6/2000

Order No. JH/1009

Item Required	Quantity	Unit price	Ref.	Total price
Vanilla ice-cream (large box)	10 boxes	£3.25	CL/234	£32.50
Strawberry ice-cream (large box)	10 boxes	£4.10	CL/235	£41.00
Chocolate ice-cream without nuts	5 boxes	£4.20	CL/237	£21.00

Signature: Diana Woods   VAT at 17.5. %

Light Delight will also need to order items from its suppliers, and will have to send the supplier an order form with details of what they want to buy.

LIGHT DELIGHT ICE-CREAM LTD

Unit 28 Penraven Industrial Estate
Mean Wood Road
LEEDS
LS7 2AP

Tel. No.: 0113 234543   **Order**   VAT Reg No: 680 73842 88

Date: 3/7/200

Order No. DF/1315

To: **The North Dairy Milk Products Ltd**
14 Dockland Road
Leeds
LS3 3DT

Please supply

Quantity	Description	Ref	Unit Price
10 Kg	Full fat milk powder	K/123	2.13 per kg
10 kg	Semi-skimmed milk powder	K/124	2.13 per kg
10 kg	Skimmed milk powder	K/125	2.13 per kg

Delivery: asap
Signed by *Renata Ottolini*

ACTIVITY

Several items of office stationery are required for the stationery counter at Light Delight Ltd. The required items are included in a memo from Gillian Ward to Renata Ottolini.

Emma Jebson, the other administration clerk, asks you to order the above items and gives you a blank order form (your tutor will give you a photocopy of the order from the back of the book). She asks you to make sure that:

MEMO

To: Renata Ottolini

From: Gillian Ward

Can you please arrange for the following items to be ordered as soon as possible from Business Supplier Ltd, 14 Dockland Road, Leeds, LS3 3DT?

1   10 boxes of blue ballpoint pens (12 per box) ref. BB/3 - cost 90p per box.

2   150 A4 writing pads ref. WP/16 (10 per pack) - cost £9.50 per pack.

3   10,000 10 × 7 White envelopes ref. WE/27 at 26 per 1000.

We get a discount from the above supplier.

GW.

---

1 The name and the address of the supplier and all of the other details on the order are correct.

2 The order numbers are in sequence. The last order number was 25/125.

3 Delivery is requested as soon as possible.

4 All order forms are signed by Renata Ottolini.

ACTIVITY

Renata Ottolini gives you a copy of an order which has been received from a new customer, Frozen Food Ltd, Newhey Road, Huddersfield HD1 2PJ (see page 116). She has noticed several errors on the order but does not have time to check these in detail. She asks you to check the order against Light Delight's price list on page 114. and to make a written note

Unit 3 Finance in businesses

of any errors. After you have done that, she wants you to send a fax to Frozen Food Ltd to let them know about the errors: ask Frozen Food Ltd to get back to you to tell you what they need. Renata gives you the price list for different ice-cream flavours:

Vanilla ice-cream @ £3.25 a box (large)
Strawberry/Raspberry ice-cream @ £4.10 a box (large)
Chocolate ice-cream with nuts @ £5.10 a box (large)
Chocolate ice-cream without nuts @ £4.20 a box (large)
Banana ice-cream with nuts @ £ 5.45 a box (large)
Banana ice-cream without nuts @ £4.75 a box (large)

ACTIVITY

Renata Ottolini asks you to order a new printer from Electronic Speed Ltd, 15 Highway Park Leeds, LS3 2FE. She gives you an order form (your tutor will give you a photocopy of the Light Delight order form at the back of the book). The printer you need to order is a Desk Jet 500 printer, Ref. No. L20, retail price £355 plus VAT.

Receiving an order

Once a business order has been received the sales department in Light Delight will:

1 Find out if there is enough ice-cream in stock.

2 Inform the production department if more ice-cream needs to be made.

3 Inform the distribution department or the person who is in charge of distribution that they have to deliver the ice-cream.

4 Inform the finance department that an invoice needs to be made out.

While all of the above is happening the sales department in the business will send the customer an **acknowledgement of order** form to show that the order has been received and is progressing.

[handwritten: find errors: See p.114 left., send bank by fax]

Frozen Food Ltd

Newhey Road
Huddersfield
HD1 2PJ

Order Form

To: Light Delight Ice-Cream Ltd
     Unit 28 Penraven Industrial Estate
     Mean Wood Road
     Leeds
     LS7 2AP

From: Aisha Hassan
       Sales manager

Order No. DF/1245   Date: 4/7/2000

Quantity	Description	Cat No.	Unit Cost	Total Cost
5	Boxes of banana ice-cream without nuts (large)	CL 239	£4.25	£21.25
10	Boxes of strawberry ice-cream (large)	CL 235	£4.10	£31.00
10	Boxes of chocolate ice-cream without nuts (large)	CL 236	£5.10	£51.00
	Subtotal			£123.25
	VAT at 17.5%			£ 21.57
	Total including VAT			£144.82

Delivery: .... Signed by: ....
Authorized by: ....

[handwritten notes:]
1) Price list
2) order form
3) acknowledgement of order (supplier) (thanks letter)
4) Delivery note

116

LIGHT DELIGHT ICE-CREAM LTD

Unit 28 Penraven Industrial Estate
Mean Wood Road
LEEDS
LS7 2AP

ACKNOWLEDGEMENT OF ORDER

Date   Order No.:   Order Date

Value of order   Expected Delivery Date

Description of Order

COMMENTS

Once Light Delight receives the order form from Sava Stores, they will do their best to deliver the ice-cream as soon as possible. Once the ice-cream is delivered, Light Delight gives or sends Sava Stores a delivery note.

When North Dairy Milk Products has received the order from Light Delight they will send them the required milk powder with a delivery note.

LIGHT DELIGHT ICE-CREAM LTD

Unit 28 Penraven Industrial Estate
Mean Wood Road
LEEDS
LS7 2AP

DELIVERY NOTE

To Sava Stores   VAT REG NO 680/7384288
22 Thorncliffe Street
Fixby
Huddersfield
HD1 1GH

Your order DF/1245	Invoice date	Invoice No	Dispatch date 10/7/00
Quantity	Description	Cat No	
10 boxes	Vanilla ice-cream	CL/234	
10 boxes	Strawberry ice-cream	CL/235	
5 boxes	Chocolate ice-cream without nuts	CL/239	

Received by....... James Bond   Date: 10/7/2000

Delivery note

A delivery note is a list of the products which have been sent by a business. It can either be included with the goods being delivered or it can be sent separately by post. It is a useful document for checking the quantity and condition of the products when they are received by the purchaser. Quantities ordered are numbered so goods can be checked. The delivery note often has a space for the recipient's signature. Businesses receive delivery notes from their suppliers when they order goods, and businesses send delivery notes to customers when they send them finished products.

NORTH DAIRY MILK PRODUCTS LTD

Delivery Note

14 Dockland Road
LEEDS
LS3 3DT

Date 9/07/2000

Our Ref. 9643

To: Light Delight Ice-cream Ltd
Unit 28 Penraven Industrial Estate
Mean Wood Road
Leeds
LS7 2AP
Your order No. DF/1315

Quantity	Description	Price per kg.
10 kg	Full fat milk	£2.13
10 kg	Semi-skimmed milk	£2.13
10 kg	Skimmed milk	£2.13

Received by Emma Jebson   **Date: 19/5/2000**

ACTIVITY

On 29 March 2000, Light Delight receives the following order from one of their customers, Brown Stores Ltd. The ice-cream is going to be delivered to Brown Stores on 12 April 2000. Emma asks you to prepare a delivery note. (ask your teacher to make you a copy of a blank delivery note from the back of the book). She also asks you to make sure that:

1 The order is correct and without any errors or mistakes.
2 The name and the address of the supplier are correct and match what is on the order form.

3 The despatch or delivery date is mentioned in the note.

BROWN STORES LTD

Main Road • HALIFAX • HA1 5HG

Order Form

To:
Light Delight Ice-Cream Ltd
Unit 28 Penraven Industrial Estate
Mean Wood Road
Leeds
LS7 2AP

Delivery address:
Brown Stores Ltd
Main Road
Halifax
HA1 5HG

Date required 12/4/00   Date of order 28/3/00   Order number BS/9340

Quantity	Please supply the following	Unit Price	Total AMOUNT
5 boxes	Strawberry ice-cream	£4.10	£20.50
10 boxes	Banana ice-cream without nuts	£4.75	£47.50
15 boxes	Chocolate ice-cream without nuts	£4.20	£63.00

Remember: The order number must appear on all invoices and delivery notes

Invoice

The sales invoice is the bill, i.e. the demand for payment. Businesses receive invoices from suppliers asking for payment, they send invoices to customers at the same time as the goods. The invoice states what has been delivered, the price and terms. The 'terms' are the amount of time allowed for payment; many businesses allow 30 days from receipt of the invoice.

<table>
</table>

┌─────────────────────────────────────┐
│ **Key facts about invoices**   │
│   │
│ 1 The invoice or bill is the main document used in business. │
│   │
│ 2 It tells the business which has bought the goods what it owes and when payment is due. │
│   │
│ 3 If the invoice is sent by a supplier to a business it will be called a purchase invoice because it is sent by the supplier to the business which has made the purchase. │
│   │
│ 4 Invoices must be paid by the purchaser once they have been received from the supplier. │
└─────────────────────────────────────┘

Information in an invoice

Various items of information are included on an invoice, for example:

a quantity, type, size and colour of the products
b final total
c value added tax (VAT).
d terms of delivery, e.g. carriage paid
e the order number.

Most businesses have a system for checking each invoice against a goods received note or delivery note. For example Emma Jebson, the administration clerk at Light Delight, checked the invoice from North Dairy Milk Products against (below left) their delivery note with reference number 9643 (page 118).

On the other hand after Light Delight delivered the ice-cream to Sava Stores, they sent them the invoice below:

NORTH DAIRY MILK PRODUCTS LTD

Light Delight Ice-cream Ltd
Unit 28 Penraven Industrial Estate
Mean Wood Road
Leeds
LS7 2AP

14 Dockland Road
LEEDS
LS3 3DT

No 451   Date 10/7/2000

INVOICE

To The purchase of

10 kg of powder full fat milk	£21.30
10 kg of powder semi-skimmed milk	£21.30
10 kg of power skimmed milk	£21.30
SUBTOTAL	£63.90
VAT 17.5%	£11.18
TOTAL DUE	£75.08

E&OE

LIGHT DELIGHT ICE-CREAM LTD
Unit 28 Penraven Industrial Estate
Mean Wood Road
LEEDS
LS7 2AP

INVOICE

VAT REG NO 680/7384288

Customer Sava Stores   Customer Ref. No:
22 Thorncliffe Street   Despatch Date: 10/7/00
Fixby
Huddersfield
HD1 1GH   Invoice No: 10202
                               Date 18/7/00

Quantity	Description	Unit Price	Total
10 kg	Large boxes of Vanilla ice-cream	£3.25 a box	£32.50
10 kg	Large boxes of Strawberry ice-cream	£4.10 a box	£41.00
10 kg	Large boxes of Chocolate ice-cream without nuts	£5.10 a box	£51.00
	E&OE	Subtotal	£124.50
		VAT (17.5%)	£21.88
		Total	£146.38

Special notes in an invoice

1   The letters "E and OE" are found on every invoice and stand for **Errors and Omissions Excepted**. This means that if there are any mistakes or items missed off, the supplier has the right to send a **supplementary invoice** to charge the extra amount still owing.

2   **Value Added Tax (VAT)** is added to the total cost of the goods (after any discounts have been subtracted). The current rate is 17.5%.

How to work out VAT in an invoice

The invoice on the previous page, sent by Light Delight Ice-cream to their customer Sava Stores, shows you how VAT is worked out.

1   The subtotal of the invoice is £124.50 (no discount is offered).

2   VAT on goods is 17.5% of £124.50 = £21.88

3   Total amount due is £124.50+ £21.88 = £146.38

Remember that sometimes businesses give a discount to encourage prompt payment. For example, in the above invoice Light Delight Ice-Cream might offer Sava Stores a 10% discount off the subtotal if payment is made within 14 days. Therefore, if Sava Stores pays quickly, the total amount which they will have to pay will be less. Look at the invoice at the top of the right-hand column.

LIGHT DELIGHT ICE-CREAM LTD

Unit 28 Penraven Industrial Estate
Mean Wood Road
LEEDS
LS7 2AP

INVOICE

VAT REG NO 680/7384288

Customer Sava Stores
22 Thorncliffe Street
Fixby
Huddersfield
HD1 1GH

Customer Ref. No:
Despatch Date: 10/7/00

Invoice No: 10202
Date 18/7/00

Quantity	Description	Unit Price	Total
10 kg	Large boxes of Vanilla ice-cream	£3.25 a box	£32.50
10 kg	Large boxes of Strawberry ice-cream	£4.10 a box	£41.00
10 kg	Large boxes of Chocolate ice-cream without nuts	£5.10 a box	£51.00
	E&OE	Subtotal	£124.50
		Discount 10%	£12.45
		Amount after discount	£112.05
		VAT (17.5%)	£19.60
		Total	£131.65

ACTIVITY: WORK IT OUT YOURSELF

In each of the following situations, calculate the final cost of the goods.

a   6 bottles @ £35.75 per bottle with 6% trade discount + VAT.

b   5 cartons @ £31.15 per carton with 10% trade discount + VAT.

c   8 dozen @ £58 per dozen with 8% trade discount + VAT.

HW 4/5

ACTIVITY: WORKING OUT VAT IN AN INVOICE

Look at the invoice below and work out:
a The amount of VAT
b The subtotal
c The total amount due.

1 Remember that there is a 5% cash discount if the invoice is paid within 10 days.
2 Follow the same steps which are shown above.

HW 5/3

ACTIVITY

On 15/4/00 Renata Ottolini at Light Delight asks you to invoice Brown Stores for the ice-cream which was delivered on 12/4/00. The order number is BS/9340. There is a discount of 12.5% for prompt payment (ask your teacher to give you a blank copy of an invoice). Renata has asked you to write and carefully check the invoice before you have it signed and authorised. She has also drawn your attention to the following components, e.g. **goods, terms, date, amount of money etc.** Before you have the invoice signed, check the following.

LIGHT DELIGHT ICE-CREAM LTD

Unit 28 Penraven Industrial Estate
Mean Wood Road
LEEDS
LS7 2AP

Bill

INVOICE

VAT REG NO 680/7384288

Customer Frozen Food Ltd Newhey Road Huddersfield HD1 2PJ	**Customer Ref. No:** **Despatch Date:** 14/8/00 **Invoice No:** 10231 **Date** 24/8/00

Quantity	Description	Unit Price	Total
15	Large boxes of Vanilla ice-cream	£3.25 a box	
5	Large boxes of Strawberry ice-cream	£4.10 a box	
10	Large boxes of Chocolate ice-cream with nuts	£5.10 a box	
7	Large boxes of Banana ice-cream without nuts	£4.75 a box	
E&OE	Subtotal Discount 5% Amount after discount VAT (17.5%) Total		

Invoice checking procedure

Component	What to check	How to check it
Name of business	Brown Stores Ltd	Their order form and delivery note
Address of business	Brown stores Ltd, Main Road Halifax HA1 5HG	Their order form and delivery note
Delivery address	Does it relate to your business Brown Stores?	Ask and check files (order form and delivery note)
Order no.	Does this match their order number?	Check against order
Despatch date	Whether the goods have been delivered	Check the Delivery Note
Quantity	Has the right quantity been delivered?	Check Goods Received Note or Delivery Note
Description of catalogue no.	Is this what they ordered?	Check order form
Price	Is this as quoted?	Check quotation or order

Component	What to check	How to check it
Total price	Are calculations accurate?	Check them!
Trade discount	Is this the discount agreed?	Check quotation or order
VAT rate	Is this correct/is VAT calculation correct?	Work it out
Delivery charges	Are you liable to pay these?	Check quotation or order

ACTIVITY

Explain in your own words what would happen if you sent the wrong invoice to Brown Stores Ltd.

Settling an invoice or account (making payment)

When businesses send an invoice or a statement of account, they like payment to be made as soon as possible. Sometimes customers are given a period of time (2–3 weeks, for example) to send this payment. As was explained above, in the process of making purchases businesses agree that immediate cash is the most favourable option or method of paying a bill! However, there are other options available to customers, e.g. cheques, credit, hire purchase etc.

Whenever payment is made, there will be a system for recording the amount and the date. This system provides evidence that the transactions have occurred and can be used to check against other financial records.

One of the most common payment methods is the cheque and you will find that most businesses use cheques a lot. The following pages will tell you how to write cheques and what happens when a business receives a cheque. You will find out about other methods of making and receiving payments on pages 141–145.

Cheques

Cheques provide a favoured method of paying bills and are one of the most common forms of payment. Businesses generally count payment by cheques as a 'cash sale' because they receive money into their bank account as soon as the cheque has been cleared. Businesses also send payment to other businesses by cheque.

A cheque is simply a written instruction from a customer to a bank to pay a certain sum of money to another named person. If you pay by cheque for something which you are going to take out of a shop straight away, then the shopkeeper takes it on trust that you have the money in your account so that the cheque will be paid.

For more expensive goods, you may have to wait for the cheque to be 'cleared' (i.e. the money transferred from your account to the retailer's). This usually takes about five days.

On the above cheque there are the names of two people:

1 The person who is paying the cheque. He/She is called the **Drawer**.

2 The person to whom the cheque is payable to (the receiver of the money). He or she is called the **Payee**.

The drawer's bank (the bank where the person who is paying for the cheque has his account) is called the **Drawee**.

Drawee

payee

SPENDALOT BANK PLC   Date *6 September 2000*   25-72-10   *bank no.*

Pay *Cheap Sports Ltd*   or order

£ *29.99*

Twenty-nine pounds and ninety-nine

pence only   *Patrick O'Brien*

538125 25 7210: 1 6213338   PATRICK O'BRIEN   *Drawer*

checkno. Bankno. accountno.

What a cheque looks like

How to safeguard a cheque

The most common way of safeguarding a cheque is to cross it, by drawing or printing two vertical or sloping lines across its face. This means that the cheque can only be paid into a bank account of the payee, and not in cash across the counter by anyone.

1 Is the above cheque well safeguarded? Explain your answer.

2 Who is the account holder?

3 At what bank is the account held?

4 What is the cheque being used for?

5 There are numbers which can be read on the above cheque?

   a Which of these numbers is the account number?

   b Which of these numbers is the cheque number?

   c Which of these numbers is the bank or the branch identifying number?

ACTIVITY

Imagine that your friend has sold you his second-hand computer game for £25.75.

1 Ask your teacher to run you 2 copies of the blank cheque at the back of your book.

2 Fill in the blank spaces in the cheque to instruct your bank to pay your friend £25.75

When writing a cheque you must remember to:

1 **Write** the date in full.

2 **Write** the payee's name (in full) clearly on the top line.

3 **Write** the amount to the left of the lines to make alterations or addition difficult.

4 **Add** the word 'only' after writing the amount.

5 **Write** the amount of pence in figures.

6 **Write** the amount in words so that it is the same as the amount in figures.

6 **Cancel** any blank spaces remaining by drawing a line through them.

7 **Sign** the cheque.

Cheque guarantee cards

If you pay for something in a shop with a cheque, the shop assistant will usually ask to see your cheque guarantee card. The assistant will write the card number on the back of the cheque and check that the card has not expired (i.e. is still in date).

A cheque guarantee card gives the shopkeeper a guarantee that the bank will pay the shop the amount written on the cheque, up to the amount the cheque guarantee card says – usually £50 or £100.

ACTIVITY

1   Why do you think shopkeepers should not accept a cheque without a guarantee card?
2   Ask someone who has recently paid for some goods with a cheque the following questions:
   a   Did the checkout operator or the sale assistant at the shop ask them to present the guarantee card?
   b   Where did the checkout operator write the number of the card on the cheque?
      On the reverse side.
      On the top corner of the front side.
      On the bottom corner of the front side.

ACTIVITY

1   Find out the type of information which is printed on the front of a cheque guarantee card.
2   Find out what is on the back of this card.

ACTIVITY

Find out if the following statements are true or false:

When writing a cheque:

1   Customers can use either a pencil or a pen. F
2   Customers should write the amount in words and figures as close to the left as possible. T
3   Customers don't have to sign against any alteration. F

4   Only one line should be drawn after the name of the person, to whom the cheque has to be paid.

ACTIVITY

Renata Ottolini at Light Delight Ltd passes you two invoices which she wants you to check. She wants you to check the calculations on the invoices. If they are correct then you have to make out a cheque for the amount due. Use today's date, then pass it to Ismat Niaz (the Finance Manager) for signature and authorisation.

If any of the invoices is incorrect, note the details in a brief memo to Renata Ottolini.

Delta Plastic Manufacture

23 River land Road
Leeds
LS2 1JB

Light Delight Ltd,   VAT Reg 456 543
Unit 28,
Penraven   Invoice no 4765
Industrial Estate,   Date 30/11/00
Mean Wood Road
Leeds
LS7 2AP

INVOICE

12 plastic packaging boxes (small)	£50.00
12 plastic packaging boxes (medium)	£70.00
12 plastic packaging boxes (large)	£95.00
Subtotal	£225.00
Plus VAT (17.5%)	£39.38
Total Due	£274.75
E&OE	

KEITH PLUMBING

17 Greenaway Rd
Leeds
LS4 6HD

INVOICE

Light Delight Ltd,   VAT Reg 225 762
Unit 28,   Invoice no 446
Penraven Industrial Estate, Date 30/11/00
Meanwood Road
Leeds
LS7 2AP

INVOICE

TO

Replacing leaking radiators:

1 600mm *2000 mm radiator	£83.25
1 600mm *1000 mm radiator	£50.90
1 thermostatic radiator valve	£7.25
7 hours @ £10.50 per hour	£5.50 73.50
Subtotal	£136.90
VAT 17.5%	£23.96
TOTAL DUE	£160.86

E&OE

ACTIVITY

Describe what would happen if you wrote the cheque to Keith Plumbing Ltd without first checking the invoice number 446.

ACTIVITY: SPOT THE ERROR

Emma Jebson is a new clerk in the administration department at Light Delight Ice-cream Ltd. Emma's main job is to receive and check the cheques which suppliers send the company to pay for the ice-cream they have purchased. In her first few weeks Emma found the work difficult and confusing. On a few occasions she was not sure if she was doing things right. The Administration Manager Renata Ottolini called Emma to her office to draw her attention to some errors.

Emma was not told what she did wrong in each of the following situations. Your task is to find the error(s) which Emma has made and to tell her what she should have done instead.

1 On 1/2/00 Emma accepted a cheque value £57.89 with no signature.
2 On 13 April 2000 Emma accepted a cheque from a customer which is dated the 13/6/1998.
3 On 23/5/00 Emma accepted a cheque from a customer with the amount of money, 75.99p. Nothing was written on the back of the cheque. guarantee no.
4 On 2/5/00 Emma accepted a cheque for £57.95, which does not have a payee's name.
5 On 7/5/00 Emma accepted a cheque with the written words for the amount Twenty three pounds and 95p. The amount in figures was £7.95.
6 On 8/5/00 Emma accepted a cheque for £65.95. Jean wrote the guarantee card number on the front side of the cheque.
7 On 16 May 2000 Emma accepted a cheque for £72.12. She wrote the card number 0002346567 and the expiry date 30/4/00 on the back of the cheque.

ACTIVITY

One Monday morning Renata is worried that some of the following cheques (all payable to Light Delight) have not been checked properly. Renata asks you to:

1 Check the following cheques.
2 Note any errors and,

3 **Advise** her what action she should take in each case.

Luckily the cheques were accepted with a cheque guarantee card.

Happy Bank plc
Date 2/7/00   92-12-20
Pay Light Delight Ltd   or order
One hundred and thirty-two   £ 123.95
pounds and ninety-five pence only
243620 92 1220: 1 1436789   SAVA STORES

Northern BANK PLC
Date 7/7/00   67-22-15
Pay Light Delight Ltd   or order
Two hundred and one pounds and   £ 201.45
forty-five pence only
172235 67 2215: 1 7533826   FROZEN FOOD LTD

Happy Bank plc
Date 4/9/00   92-12-20
Pay Light Delight Ltd   or order
Sixty-seven pounds and seventy-   £ 76.67
six pounds only
243621 92 1220: 1 1436789   SAVA STORES

Northern BANK PLC
Date 4/10/01   67-22-15
Pay Light Delight Ltd   or order
One hundred and thirty-two and   £ 96.63
95p only
172235 67 2215: 1 7533826   FROZEN FOOD LTD

ACTIVITY

The following week Renata asks you to write and sign all of the following cheques, using today's date (print out copies of the blank cheque at the back of the book):

1 A cheque for £42.65 payable to North Dairy Milk Products Ltd.
2 A cheque for £238.29 payable to Speed Manufacturer Ltd.
3 A cheque for £89.98 payable to Juicy Fruity Ltd.
4 A cheque for £101.10 payable to Keith Plumbing Ltd.

ACTIVITY

Because of the errors that Emma made with the cheques last week, Renata Ottolini asks you to type a note for her which states exactly what procedure should be followed when accepting cheque payments.

HW

ACTIVITY

On 3/5/2000 Light Delight Ice-Cream Ltd. receives the following order from one of their regular customers, Frozen Food Ltd.

1 Check all the prices and the arithmetic on the purchase order against the price list. Correct any errors.
2 Check all the items on the delivery note against what is required in the purchase order. Correct any errors.
3 Check all the items on the invoice against the accurate copy of the delivery note.
4 If you think that the invoice is correct and should be paid, sign it and complete a cheque ready for signature.

5 If you think the invoice is not correct, make the required correction, sign it and complete a cheque ready for signature.

LIGHT DELIGHT ICE-CREAM LTD

Unit 28 Penraven Industrial Estate
Mean Wood Road
LEEDS
LS7 2AP

Selected Price List

Ice-cream

Qty	Item	Cat No	Price
Large box	Vanilla ice-cream	CL/234	£3.25
Large box	Strawberry/Rasberry ice-cream	CL/235	£4.10
Large box	Chocolate ice-cream with nuts	CL/236	£5.10
Large box	Chocolate ice-cream without nuts	CL/237	£4.20
Large box	Banana ice-cream with nuts	CL/238	£5.45
Large box	Banana ice-cream without nuts	CL/239	£4.75
Large box	Raspberry ice-cream	CL/240	£4.10

Frozen Food Ltd

Newhey Road
Huddersfield
HD1 2PJ

Order Form

To: Light Delight Ice-Cream Ltd
      Unit 28 Penraven Industrial Estate
      Mean Wood Road
      Leeds
      LS7 2AP

From: Aisha Hassan
       Sales manager

Order No. DF/1245   Date: 30/4/00

Quantity	Description	Cat No.	Unit Cost	Total Cost
15	Boxes of vanilla ice-cream	CL/234	£3.25	£48.75
10	Boxes of strawberry ice-cream (large)	CL/235	£5.10	£51.00
20	Boxes of chocolate ice-cream (large), no nuts	CL 236	£4.25	£85.00
	Total			£184.75
	VAT at 17.5%			£32.33
	Total including VAT			£217.08

Delivery: within 2 weeks
Signed by: ....
Authorized by: Aisha Hassan

The above order was delivered on 9 May 2000, and the following delivery note was issued.

LIGHT DELIGHT ICE-CREAM LTD

Unit 28 Penraven Industrial Estate
Mean Wood Road
LEEDS
LS7 2AP

DELIVERY NOTE

To: Frozen Food Ltd   VAT REG   NO 680/7384288
Newhey Road
Huddersfield
HD1 2PJ

Your order	Invoice date	Invoice No	Dispatch date
DF/1245	13/5/00		9/5/00

Quantity	Description	Cat No
15 boxes	Vanilla ice-cream	CL/234
10 boxes	Strawberry ice-cream	CL/235
20 boxes	Chocolate ice-cream with nuts	CL/236

Received by....... James Bond   Date: 9/05/200

LIGHT DELIGHT ICE-CREAM LTD

Unit 28 Penraven Industrial Estate
Mean Wood Road
LEEDS
LS7 2AP

INVOICE

VAT REG NO 680/7384288

Customer Frozen Food Ltd
Newhey Road
Huddersfield
HD1 2PJ

Customer Ref. No:
Despatch Date: 9/5/00

Invoice No: 12134
Date 13/5/00

Quantity	Description	Unit Price	Total
15	Large boxes of Vanilla ice-cream	£3.25 a box	£49.74
5	Large boxes of Strawberry ice-cream	£4.10 a box	£41.00
10	Large boxes of Chocolate ice-cream with nuts	£5.10 a box	£102.00
E&OE	Subtotal		£192.75
	Discount 5%		£9.60
	Amount after discount		£202.35
	VAT (17.5%)		£35.35
	Total		£237.70

Statement of account

Statement of account Light Delight Ice-cream Ltd usually receives a statement of account from their supplier. Sometimes suppliers send the statement at the end of each month to show what is owed and what has been paid. Light Delight also sends statements of account at the end of the month to their own regular customers, mainly supermarkets. A statement lists payments as **credits** and the amounts owed as **debits**. Opposite is a statement from Light Delight to Sava Stores.

LIGHT DELIGHT ICE-CREAM LTD

Unit 28 Penraven Industrial Estate
Mean Wood Road
LEEDS
LS7 2AP

FAX: 0113 234543   VAT REG NO 680/73842/88
TEL: 0113 234544

STATEMENT

To: **Sava Stores**
      22 Thorncliffe Street
      Fixby
      Huddersfield
      HDI IGH

Date: 31/7/2000   **Account no 2327**

Date	Details	Debit	Credit	Balance
10/7/2000	10 boxes of chocolate ice-cream (invoice number 10202)	£146.38		£146.38
22/7/2000	6 boxes of vanilla ice-cream and 4 boxes of strawberry (invoice number 10221)	£35.90		£35.90
29/7/2000	5 boxes of chocolate ice-cream with nuts (invoice number 10267)	£25.50		£25.50
Total outstanding balance				£207.78

ACTIVITY

In October 2000, Sava Stores buys the following from Light Delight:

1 2/6/00 – 8 boxes of Vanilla ice-cream at £3.25 a box.
2 13/6/00 – 12 boxes of Chocolate and nuts ice-cream at £5.10 a box.
3 26/6/00 – 6 boxes of banana ice-cream without nuts.

On 27 October Sava Stores paid £35 of their outstanding balance

Prepare a statement for October to be sent to Sava Stores using a copy of the blank statement from the back of the book. Work out their total outstanding balance.

What should a business do when it receives a statement?

When the statement is received the purchaser should check it against all invoices, credit/debit notes and payments made since the last statements, and if it is correct send payment to the supplier.

What happens if the statement is not settled?

Settling a statement simply means sending the payment to the supplier. If the payment is not sent, the supplier will send another copy to the business (purchaser).

Light Delight receives the following statement for July from their supplier North Dairy Milk Products Ltd.

STATEMENT

NORTH DAIRY MILK PRODUCTS LTD

Light Delight Ltd,
Unit 28, Penraven
Industrial Estate,   Date 3/07/00
Meanwood Road
Leeds
LS7 2AP   Account No 668750

14 Dockland Road
LEEDS
LS3 3DT

Date	Item Description	Debits	Credits
2/7/00	5kg of full fat milk	£10.65	
	10kg of full fat milk	£21.30	
15/7/00	payment received thank you		£10.65
19/7/00	20kg of fat free milk	£42.60	
23/7/00	7kg of semi skimmed milk	£14.91	
Total outstanding balance			**£78.80**

£78.81

Payment received after 30 July is not included

ACTIVITY

Check the above statement to make sure that the outstanding balance is correct.

ACTIVITY

The following transaction took place in September 2000 between Light Delight Ltd and its customer Frozen Food Ltd. The customer account number is 2355.

1 Use a blank copy of the Light Delight statement to record the following transactions.
2 Work out the total outstanding balance at the end of the month.
  a 4/9/00 Frozen Food Ltd bought 15 large boxes of Chocolate ice-cream flavour without nuts @ £4.20 a box
  b 12/9/00 Frozen Food Ltd bought 8 large boxes of Vanilla ice-cream @ £3.20 a box.
  c 27/9/00 payment of £60.00 was received from Frozen Food Ltd.
  d 29/9/00 Frozen Food Ltd bought another 5 large boxes of vanilla ice-cream.

Remittance advice slips

The supplier will send businesses a document called a remittance advice slip at the same time as a statement of account. It is often attached to the statement.

The remittance advice slip is designed to be detached from the statement and returned with the payment. It gives details of how

to pay the balance of the account (the amount that is owed).

Just as businesses receive remittance advice from suppliers and other businesses, which they return with the payment, they go through the same process with customers. Businesses also send a remittance advice slip to customers at the same time as a statement of account. It is often attached to the customer's statement of account.

Customers should detach the remittance advice slip from the statement of account and return it with the payment.

A remittance advice slip generally includes the account number and address to which payment must be sent.

REMITTANCE ADVICE

Ref No 2232

Please send payment to: Customer name:

LIGHT DELIGHT ICE-CREAM LTD

Unit 28 Penraven Industrial Estate
Mean Wood Road
LEEDS
LS7 2AP

Customer Account No: Cheque:................................

Amount due: Cash:................................

                                        Total amount paid..............

 ACTIVITY

Sava Stores sends Light Delight their outstanding balance for July (go back to the July statement on page 129). Obtain a blank copy of the remittance advice slip (at the back of your book) and fill it in.

Why do you think it is useful to return this document with payment to Light Delight?

Evidence of payment: receipts

When a customer pays for goods or a service, a receipt is provided. A copy of the receipt is kept for the supplier's own records and this receipt is also the customer's evidence of paying for the product, and it proves his or her ownership of the product.

A receipt is vital if goods have to be returned; otherwise the supplier might refuse to accept them.

Businesses might provide customers with one of the following receipts.

Hand-written receipts

This is usually the case with small businesses that do not have the facility to make printed receipts. Looking at the receipt below, it was issued by the Light Delight business to their customer Sava Stores in settlement of the invoice number 10202.

> **LIGHT DELIGHT ICE-CREAM LTD**
> Unit 28 Penraven Industrial Estate
> Mean Wood Road
> LEEDS
> LS7 2AP
>
> **RECEIPT**   No 121
>
> RECEIVED FROM: _Sava Stores_
>
> _the sum of one hundred and forty six_
>
> _pounds and 37p_   _£146.37_
>
> _the payment of invoice number 10202_
>
> _Received by Emma. J   Date 17/7/00_

Printed receipts

These are usually printed out by a cash register and are offered to customers by large businesses, e.g. supermarkets, retailers and petrol stations. Receipts usually show the following information:

- date
- the number of items which were purchased
- how they were purchased
- the name of the store or the shop
- any discount the customer received.

> **RECEIPT**   **NORTH DAIRY MILK PRODUCTS LTD**
>
> 14 Dockland Road
> LEEDS
> LS3 3DT
>
> Number: 7001   Date: 15/7/00
>
> Received from: Light Delight Ice-cream Ltd
>
> The sum of: Ten pounds and thirty p only.
>
>   £10.65   sixty five
>
> For: milk powder

RECEIPT

NORTH DAIRY MILK PRODUCTS LTD

14 Dockland Road
LEEDS
LS3 3DT

Number: 7002   Date: 1/8/00

Received from: Light Delight Ice-cream Ltd

The sum of: Forty-six pounds and sixty p only.

£40.65   *not same*

For: milk powder

ACTIVITY: READING RECEIPTS

Read carefully the information on the above receipt

1   Which business issued this receipt?
2   Why was the receipt issued?
3   What other information can you read there?

ACTIVITY

1   Renata Ottolini gives you blank copies of the business receipt (ask your tutor for a copy of the receipt from the back of the book) and asks you to write and send the two receipts for the settlement of the following payments:

   a   payment of £60.00 received from Frozen Food Ltd on 27/9/00
   b   payment of £35.90 received from Sava Stores on 3/8/00.

2   Check the two receipts received from North Dairy Milk Products on page 131 and 132. Can you spot any errors?

ACTIVITY

Brown Stores Ltd sent a cheque on 23/4/00 to pay for their order no. BS/9340. The ice-cream was delivered on 12/4/00. In previous activities you have prepared and sent them a delivery note and an invoice. Renata Ottolini asks you to write and send a receipt to acknowledge that payment has been received (ask your teacher for a blank copy).

ACTIVITY

Collect three different receipts from different businesses for three different products, which you or your family have purchased in the last few weeks. What information can you find on each receipt?

Receipts	Information

Draw a table like the one above. Stick the three receipts on it and write down the relevant information which is included on each one.

ACTIVITY

Brown Stores is a regular customer of Light Delight. On 4 March 2000 they buy 2 boxes of vanilla ice-cream at £3.25 a box and a box of chocolate ice-cream at £4.20 a box. On 25 May they pay the total amount due by cheque. Renata Ottolini asks you to check the following cheque – if it is correct, write and send Brown Stores a receipt (you can ask your tutor to photocopy a blank receipt from the back of the book)

☺ SMILEY BANK PLC	Date_____30–87–12
Pay —Light Delight Ltd	or order
Ten pounds and 70p only	£ 10.70
1356 30 8712: 1 7654221 BROWN STORES	

If you think that the cheque is not correct, make the required correction and write a receipt.

Credit notes

When a customer is overcharged or returns unsuitable or damaged products, a credit note may be issued by the supplier.

* Credit notes let the purchaser know that he or she is entitled to a full refund of the cost of the returned items.

* Credit notes give the customer the right to spend at a future date in the shop (for some businesses a credit note must be used within 3 months).

* It is within the customer's rights to refuse the credit note and insist on a cash refund if the goods are faulty.

For example, the following credit note was issued by North Dairy Products Ltd. on 1/10/00. Light Delight ordered 10kg of fat-free milk. The wrong order was delivered. Therefore, a credit note with the amount of £21.30 was issued.

CREDIT NOTE	NORTH DAIRY MILK PRODUCTS LTD
Valid for 3 months	14 Dockland Road LEEDS LS3 3DT
Number: 543 **Date:** 3/9/00	
To: Light Delight Ice-cream Ltd	
The sum of: Twenty one pounds and thirty p only.	
Reasons: delivery of wrong order.	
Signature: Ali Akram	

ACTIVITY

Discuss with your partner if the customer has the right to refuse a credit note and to insist on a cash refund in the following situations:

1 Mary has recently bought new dress, without trying it on in the store. When she got home she realised that the dress was too small.
2 Carly received a brown leather handbag as a present from her husband on her birthday. Carly did not like the colour and wants to exchange it for a black one.
3 John recently bought a pair of pyjamas. When he washed them for the first time, at the right temperature, they shrunk.

4   Louise bought a new pair of shoes two months ago. After she wore them only a few times the heel wore out.

HW
15/5

ACTIVITY

Sava Stores orders five boxes of vanilla ice-cream from Light Delight Ltd at £3.25 a box. When the order is delivered, Hussain Ahmed, the owner of the supermarket, finds that it is the wrong flavour. He telephones Light Delight to complain. Louise, the Customer Service Manager at Light Delight, is very understanding and apologises to him for this error. She tells him that she will send him a credit note including £5 extra as an apology. Louise asks you to write the note immediately and send it to Sava Stores with a letter of apology. (Ask your teacher to provide you with a blank Light Delight credit note from the back of the book.)

ACTIVITY: THE PURCHASE AND SALE PROCESS

You have learned from the information above that businesses need to make purchases and sales when they trade with suppliers and customers. In this trading process of buying and selling, more or less the same documents are used. When businesses buy from a supplier they receive financial documents and when they sell to customers they send them.

WORD
Customers
Purchase
Send invoice
Make payment

OPPOSITE
Sell
Receive payment
Receive delivery note
Suppliers

Send statement   Receive invoice
Send delivery note   Receive statement

1   Match each of the above words/processes with the opposite one.
2   Rearrange some of the above words into two main headings:
    a   The purchases process for a business.
    b   The sales process for a business.
3   Write in the right order the financial documents which a business sends or receives when it purchases goods from a supplier.
4   Write in the right order the financial documents which a business sends or receives when it sells goods to a customer.

Some businesses purchase (buy in) goods from suppliers to sell them to customers. Others purchase raw materials and equipment to make and sell a final product.

There are two flows: goods flow into the business and goods flow out of the business.

In these buying and selling transactions there are two processes:

a   The process of making purchases.

b   The process of making sales.

ACTIVITY

Fill in the gaps in the following statements by using only opposite words to the underlined ones (use the opposites from the activity above).

The first one is done for you.

1   The first stage of a <u>purchase</u> process is to <u>place</u> an order with a <u>supplier</u>.

The first stage of a <u>selling</u> process is to <u>receive</u> an order from a <u>customer</u>.

Word	Opposite
purchase	selling
deliver	receive
suppliers	customers

2   The second stage of a **purchase** process is to **receive** goods and a delivery note

The second stage of a ...*selling*... process is to *deliver* goods to customers and a delivery note.

3   The third stage of a **purchase** process is to **receive** an invoice.

The third stage of a ...*selling*... process is to *deliver* an invoice.

4   The fourth stage of a **purchase** process is to **receive** a statement of account with remittance slip.

The fourth stage of a ...*selling*... process is to *deliver* a statement of account with remittance slip.

5   The fifth stage of a **purchase** process is to **make** payment and to **send back** the remittance slip.

The fifth stage of a ...*selling*... process is to *deliver* payment and *deliver* the remittance slip.

SAME

5   The final stage of a **purchase** process is to **make** payment and **to send back** the remittance slip.

The final stage of a ...*selling*... process is to *deliver* payment and *deliver* the remittance slip.

ACTIVITY

Draw two separate charts to illustrate the financial documents, which are used with Light

Delight Ltd in their purchases process from a supplier and sale processes to a customer.

ACTIVITY: PURCHASE OR SALES!

As you have already learnt, the following documents record the financial transactions for the purchases function or the sales function.

Financial documents:

- order (purchase order form)
- delivery note
- invoice
- statement of account
- remittance advice
- cheque
- receipt

This activity will help you to understand when the each of these documents is used in the two business processes of making a purchase and making a sale.

Fill in the gaps in the following sentences using only one of two words, **sale** or **purchase**.

1   When a business **receives** a delivery note, this is a step in the process of making a ...*P*... .

2   When a business **sends** an invoice, this is a step in the process of making a ...*S*... .

3   When a business **sends** a statement of account, this is a step in the process of making a ...*S*... .

4   When a business **sends** a customer a receipt, this is a step in the process of making a ...*S*... .

5   When a business **receives** a remittance advice, this is a step the process of making a ...*P*... .

6 When a business **sends** a cheque out to settle an account, this is the final step in the process of making a ....

7 When a business **sends** a purchase order form, this is a step in the process of making a ....

8 When a business **receives** a delivery note, this is a step in the process of making a ....

9 When a business **receives** a receipt from a supplier, this is a step in the process of making a ....

Petty cash vouchers

Most offices find that they need to make cash payments each day for items bought for the office, e.g. cleaning materials, light bulbs, tea, coffee, flowers and plants. Instead of asking the chief cashier each time cash is required, it is simpler to make these payments from petty cash.

What is the petty cash?

The petty cash is an amount of money made up of small notes and coins. This cash is kept in a lockable metal cash box.

It is sensible to have only one set of keys for the cash box and these keys are generally looked after by an accounts clerk or a senior secretary. The person may also be called the petty cashier.

What is a petty cash voucher?

Whenever an employee wishes to claim back money which has been spent on items for the office, they should complete a petty cash voucher with details of the items

purchased and the price paid. Receipts should always be obtained for these items and attached to the petty cash voucher as proof of purchase.

Petty cash voucher	No 103	
	Date: 13/2/00	
For what required	**Amount**	
	£	**P**
2 pints of fresh milk		75
2 cartons of fresh apple juice	1	98
Sandwiches for the Director's meeting	12	43
Total Cash Spending	15	16
VAT is included		
Signature Emma. J		
Authorised R. Ottolini		

Example of a petty cash voucher

Petty cash items are usually quite small purchases. Even so, the total amount of petty cash expenditure in a business over a year can be considerable.

This is particularly true for a large company with many employees. For every petty cash purchase, a petty cash voucher must be completed. Even for very small purchases (for example, of 50p or less), on each petty cash voucher a note should be made as to whether or not the price paid included VAT.

If more than one item has been purchased, the amounts are totalled on the voucher to show the full amount being claimed. The voucher should be dated and signed by the person claiming the money.

Jess!!!

Things to remember about petty cash vouchers:

1 The receipts should be kept and attached to the voucher as proof of purchase and the amount of money spent.

2 The voucher would also be completed by the petty cashier before making payments to people who were being paid for a service they had given the company, e.g. milkman, cleaner and window cleaner.

3 All vouchers are numbered and should be issued in numerical order

4 The vouchers are usually issued before the money is spent.

5 Junior staff must obtain authorisation from a supervisor before spending any money on behalf of the company or claiming any money from the petty cash.

6 Completed vouchers must be filed safely in numerical or date order.

 # ACTIVITY

On 3 August 2000 John Edward who works as a secretary in the company ordered some sandwiches (£8.98), 4 cartons of fruit juice (£2.97) and some fresh flowers (£1.99) for the Board of Directors meeting.

Petty cash voucher	No 1
	Date:
For what required	**Amount** £ P
Total Cash Spending	
VAT is included	
Signature	....
Authorised	....

Agreed by senior person
Signed by.

Fill in a copy of the petty cash voucher below, and consider the following:

1 What information should be filled in?
2 What is John's total spending? *13.94*
3 Who should sign the above voucher? *J. Edward.*
4 Who could authorise the above voucher?
   agree

Checking petty cash vouchers

The petty cashier will check that the voucher has been correctly completed (dated, added up correctly, signed, authorised) and is supported by receipts for the purchase.

The petty cashier numbers the vouchers, in order, and they are filed in numerical order. The cash can then be handed over to the person making the claim.

Where petty cash vouchers are kept

All completed vouchers must be kept with the petty cash box as they will be needed at a later date when the petty cash is checked and balanced.

Question
Why do you think it is important that the petty cash voucher is completed and signed by the petty cashier before the money is given out?

 # ACTIVITY

Renata Ottolini the Administration manager at Light Delight Ltd asks you to work out how much money should remain in the petty cash tin on the date given, and should be reported to the petty cashier:

1 3/11/00 – petty cash amount £100. *float £50.05*
  Vouchers paid out to date: £26.25, £4.50,
  £12.75, 95p, £3.35, £2.25. *£49.95 = vouchers*
2 4/11/98 – petty cash amount £50. Vouchers
  paid out to date: £17.25, £3.50, £1.75, 80p,
  £10.35, £7.25. *£9.10 float, £40.90 vouchers*
3 10/11/98 – petty cash amount £25.
  Vouchers paid out to date: £8.15, £5.50,
  £2.25, £1.05, £5.35, 75p. *1.95 float, £23.05*

 ACTIVITY

Renata asks you to complete a pretty cash
voucher for cleaning materials at £7.50 and
sugar for the office at £2.54. The amount in
the petty cash tin is £25, and she tells you
that the last petty cash voucher number was
3454.

1 Who should sign this voucher? *~~boss~~ Renata*
2 Who should authorise this voucher? *boss*
3 How much money should remain in the
  petty cash tin at the end of the day? *£14.96*

 ACTIVITY

Renata Ottolini gives Emma £40 from the
petty cash. Emma spends most of the money
on mailing two parcels, buying fresh milk,
computer disks and stationery items. Renata
asks you to check the following cash/petty
voucher before she authorises it. Find out how
much money Emma should have left.

£9.30

Petty cash voucher		No 776
		Date: **29/9/00**
For what required	**Amount**	
	£	**P**
fee for mailing 2 parcels	7	20
2 pints of fresh milk	0	75
computer disks	12	40
stationery items	10	35
Total Cash Spending	35	07
VAT is included		*30 7⁰*
Signature	*Emma. J*	
Authorised		

 17/5 HW

ACTIVITY: WHAT KIND OF DOCUMENT AM I?

You have learned that businesses use a variety
of financial documents when sales and
purchases are made. Each of these documents
is simply a piece of paper with some
important information. The name and the
description of this piece of paper depends on:
1 **the nature** and type of written
  information
2 **the purpose** of this information
3 **the user** of the information.

In this activity you have to find out the proper
name for each of the following pieces of paper.
The description of the information will help
you to identify the document

Before you do the activity revise the terms at
the end of this unit.

1 *I am a document* which firms have to
  complete and send to a supplier to order

or buy a product. I contain full details of the quantity, type, size and colour of the goods required. *Order Form*

2   *I am a document* with a written order or instruction from someone to a bank to pay a specific sum of money to someone else. *Cheque*

3   *I am a document* which is issued by a business to a customer. I entitle the buyer of the product to a full refund of the cost of returned items, e.g. damaged items. *Credit notes*

4   *I am a document* which is carried by the driver of a delivery vehicle. I am a list of the products which have been sent by a supplier. *delivery notes.*

5   *I am a document* which tells the business that has bought the goods what it owes and when payment is due. I am sent at the same time as the goods. I state what has been delivered, the price and terms. *Invoice*

6   *I am a document* which must be completed when a petty cash purchase is made. *pretty cash voucher*

7   *I am a document* which is sent by a business at the same time as a statement of account. I am often attached to the statement. I include details, e.g. account number, customer's name etc. *Remittance advice slips*

8   *I am a document* which provides a customer with evidence that they have paid for a product, and proves his or her ownership of it. *receipt.*

9   *I am a document* which shows a business what it is owed and what it has been paid. I list payments as credits and the amounts owed as debits. *statement*

ACTIVITY: WHY KEEP FINANCIAL DOCUMENTS?

22/5 Homework

All businesses need to record, store and keep information about their suppliers and their customers. This activity will help you to understand why a business needs to store these financial documents that were used to make sales or purchases.

1   Find out if each of the following statements is **true** or **false**.

a   Businesses record and keep financial information about customers and suppliers in order to be able to work out how much they spend and how much they owe them. *T*

b   Keeping sufficient and accurate information and records about suppliers helps businesses to receive and organise customers' orders. *T*

c   Keeping sufficient and accurate information and records about customers helps businesses to work out their needs and wants. *F/T*

d   Keeping sufficient and accurate information and records about customers helps businesses to order the right level of stock from suppliers. *T*

e   Keeping sufficient and accurate information and records about suppliers helps businesses to work out their expenditure (spending) on suppliers. *F*

f   Keeping sufficient and accurate information and records about suppliers helps businesses to work out their income from sales. *F*

g   Keeping information about customers does not help businesses to communicate with them. *F*

h   Keeping information about suppliers helps businesses to offer a better customer service and after-sale service. *F*

i   Keeping sufficient and accurate information about customers wastes a business's time and resources in working out and claiming outstanding balances. F

j   Keeping adequate information and records about suppliers helps business to satisfy customers' needs and wants. T / F

£1000 on access bill.
① Pay the full amount.
② Pay the minimum amount £
③ Pay any amount over the minimum

Methods of making and receiving payments

When you go to a supermarket to do your weekly shopping, or a shop to buy clothes or to a restaurant to buy a meal, usually you can pay for what you buy in different ways. Perhaps the most common ways nowadays to pay for what we buy are:

- cash
- cheques
- charge cards
- credit cards
- debit cards.

Cash

As we have said before, businesses agree that immediate cash is the most favoured method to pay a bill. The retailer gets the money immediately. Although cash is becoming less important it is still needed to make certain low-value purchases, for example, buying sweets or a newspaper from a corner shop.

Buying with a card

There are many different types of plastic cards but they all use a similar system at the point of sale – the situation where, having decided what you want to buy, you bring out a piece of plastic to pay for it!

The cashier or sales assistant will fill out a sales voucher which shows details of what you have bought and how much it cost. You hand over your card and the coded information on it is imprinted on to the sales voucher. In some cases this can be done electronically.

You check that the details are correct and then sign. A copy is given to you and this is your record that you have spent that money.

The shop or business from whom you bought the goods will make a number of sales during the day where people have paid with the same type of card as you used. They send all the sales vouchers off to the company which runs the card and at the end of the month they will be paid for all the sales made.

The card company sorts out all the vouchers belonging to your card number, and at the end of the month you will receive a state-ment showing all the purchases made using your card and the total amount you owe.

What you do now depends upon the type of card and how you are choosing to use it.

Charge cards

With a charge card, when you get your statement at the end of the month you have to pay the amount owing. Examples of charge cards are American Express and Diners Card.

Debit cards

Debit cards are used in the same way as cheques. The best known systems are called

Switch, Connect and Delta. Before the payment is made the checkout operator checks to see if there are sufficient funds in the customer's account.

The transaction requires the customer's own signature on the sales voucher to prevent fraud.

? Did you know?

Some debit cards like Barclays Connect can not only be used as a debit card but also as a £100 cheque guarantee card, which allows you to withdraw money from thousands of cash machines in the UK and many more worldwide.

Credit cards

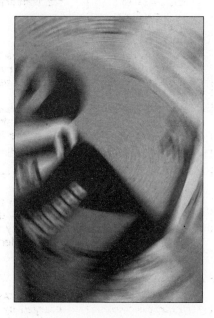

The best known credit cards are Access and Visa. With credit cards, customers buy the product now and pay later. Immediate payment is not required.

Once you are 18 or over, you can apply for a credit card.

With a credit card such as Access you are given a spending limit when you apply. When you receive your statement at the

end of the month, you can if you wish pay off all the balance outstanding. Your statements will show the date by which you must make the payment. If you make a purchase right at the start of your month then it may be 7 weeks before you pay the card company. In this way a credit card is rather like a free overdraft and many people use their cards in this way.

The risk of card theft and fraud is causing some banks to experiment with customer's photographs on cards.

? Did you know?

1 VisaCard and MasterCard are accepted in 14 million outlets in over 200 countries worldwide.

2 Credit cards may be used to withdraw cash at any bank branch for a small fee (£1 – £1.50).

3 There is an immediate interest charge for this service. A credit card could be used as a guarantee card.

ACTIVITY

1   Ask three different people, preferably card holders, which method(s) they usually prefer to use when they purchase goods or services. Find out why they prefer this particular method(s).

2   Which methods of payment would you prefer to use to purchase each of the following items:
   a   a packet of sweets Cash, small amount
   b   a bottle of wine debit card
   c   a piece of home furniture Credit card, large amou
   d   the supermarket weekly shopping storedt card.
   e   a winter coat credit card debit card
   f   paying a deposit for a holiday?
   cash, credit card

Explain your answers.

Annakm   Annakm   · annakm   Annakm

Store charge cards

Many major stores operate a charge card which can be used to purchase goods only in branches of the store, eg the Marks & Spencer Charge Card. It works both as a charge and a credit card. You can spend up to a certain amount and have the choice to repay in full or spread the payments over a number of months. If you don't repay in full at the end of the month then interest will be charged and added to your account.

Instant electronic payments

Banks have had to develop appropriate ways of making payments in these new systems, eg debit and credit cards. When customers hand in their cards to the shopkeepers or the checkout operators they give instructions to their bank to make payments for them via an electronic network.

Instant electronic payments using a wide range of payment and credit cards will increase. An electronic terminal reads a

Method of payment	Advantages		Disadvantages	
	Buyer	**Seller**	**Buyer**	**Seller**
Cash	• Knows how much money is left	• Gets money immediately	• Has to carry around a lot of cash, risk of losing it/being mugged etc	• Shops can become a target for robbery
Cheques	• Easy to carry around • Generally accepted	• Guaranteed up to £50 or £100 • Not attractive for robbers	• For expensive items retailer may not release goods immediately but wait until cheque has 'cleared'	• Takes about 5 days for money to reach seller's account • Cheques can 'bounce' after buyer has left with goods
Credit cards	• Easy to carry around • Not limited to amount in account • Gives some consumer protection	• Payment guaranteed (unless stolen) • Useless to robbers	• Easy to run up large debts • Easy to steal	• Credit card companies charge up to 5% • It takes – days for money to reach seller's account
Debit cards	• Easy to carry around • Spending limited to amount in account • Some stores give 'cash back'	• Payment guaranteed (unless stolen) • Usless to robbers • By giving 'cash back' can reduce amount of cash in tills • Payment instant	• Buyer is limited to amount so can't spread spending • Easy to steal	• A percentage is charged by banks to handle transaction
Store cards	• Offer the buyer 'perks' such as extra discount	• Encourages buyers to return to that store	• Rates of interest very high • Can only be used in named stores	

magnetic strip on the card when it is passed, or swiped, through it.

Can you be refused a card?

One day you might apply for a credit card or a store card and find that your bank or the business which you are applying to says no. The business or the bank has the right to refuse if they think you could be a bad risk. Your bank or the business does not have to say why, but the chances are they would have consulted a credit reference agency. There are a number of credit reference agencies throughout the country that collect information on people who may have not paid their debts in the past.

Stolen cards

Lost or stolen cards can be like losing money. But you can help to prevent other people from using your card by arranging a card protection scheme with your bank or building society. The schemes will cover all your cards, credit, debit, store and member fees cards. You can make one free call to cancel all missing cards and they will also replace the lost cards with new ones.

ACTIVITY

1 Find 3 businesses in the high street which operate a charge card system. Write down the names of these businesses or stores.
2 What is the size of each of these businesses?
3 Write to or ring the customer service department in one of these businesses. Find out about the rules for applying for a charge card, eg age, occupation, etc.
4 Find out what you have to do if the card got lost or stolen.
5 Find out if local small shops issue charge cards to their customers. Why do you think this is the case?

ACTIVITY: BE SECURE

When you become a customer of a bank you are given items like cheque books and cards to help you make payments. If they fall into the wrong hands, money could be taken from your account by somebody else. You need to look after your 'financial instruments' and here are some words of advice.

Suggest what could happen if you don't listen to each of the following:

1 **Don't keep** your cheque card in the same wallet, pocket or bag as your cheque book.
2 **Don't leave** your cheque book and your cards in a changing room or cloakroom.
3 **Don't write** your cashpoint PIN number down on to a piece of paper and keep it with your card.
4 **Don't peer** over somebody's shoulder when you are at a cash point and don't let anyone look over yours.

Other methods of payment

The above methods of payment are not the only ones which customers can use to purchase a product. There are other methods of payment which some businesses allow customers to use. Other common methods include:

Standing orders

Sometimes a customer wants to make the payment for a fixed sum at regular intervals, eg a hire purchase instalment. To avoid having to remember to make a cheque on the right date, a standing order may be given to the customer's bank.

This instructs them to transfer from your account a stated amount at regular intervals to the bank of the payee.

Hire purchase

This is an older system than credit card sales. It is very similar in that the customer has the goods and pays for them over a long period of time (up to 3 years). With the hire purchase agreement you can spread the cost of buying a product over a period of time, 6 or 12 months. Customers have to pay interest to be able to obtain the facility.

However, the customer does not become the legal owner of the goods until the last payment. If the customer fails to keep up with the payments, the goods can be repossessed.

Key Terms

Advice note A note that is sent from the supplier to the business (shop or warehouse) when an order is received.

Bank statement A statement that includes a summary of transactions over a period of time. It shows records of payments (debits) and receipts (credits).

Cheque IAn order written by the drawer (the person who writes the chequeto a bank to pay on demand a specific sum of money to someone else (the payee.

Cheque guarantee card A plastic, personal card with the name and account number of the holder and the expiry date. It guarantees that the banks will honour the cheque. There is usually a sued by a business to a customer. It entitles the buyer of the product to a full refund of the cost of returned items, e.g. damaged items.

Debit card A method of payment, e.g. Switch, Delta and Connect.

Delivery note A note that is carried by the driver of the delivery vehicle. It is a list of the products that have been sent by a supplier.

Drawee The drawer's bank where he or she holds an account.

Drawer The person writing the cheque.

Invoice A bill (demand for payment) which tells the business that has bought the goods what it owes and when payment is due. It is sent at the same time as the goods. It states what has been delivered, the price and terms.

Payee The person who receives the cheque.

Petty cash Cash that is available in a business for small purchases, e.g. coffee, sugar.

Petty cash voucher A piece of paper that must be completed when a petty cash purchase is made.

Purchase order form A form which firms have to complete and send to the supplier to order or buy a product. It contains full details of the quantity, type, size and colour of the goods required.

Receipt Customer's evidence of paying for the product, and it proves his ownership of the product.

Remittance advice A document that is send by a business at the same time as a statement of account. It is often attached to the statement. It includes details, e.g. account number, customer name etc.

Statement of account Statement that shows a business what it is owed and what it has been paid. It lists payments as credits and the amounts owed as debits.

Store charge card A card that is issued by a big store or retailer to customers, allowing them to make purchases only in that store. It acts like a credit card, so customers do not have to make immediate payment when they purchase the product. An example is Marks and Spencer Charge Card.

Value Added Tax (VAT) An indirect tax that is added to the total cost of the goods (after any discounts have been deducted). The current rate is 17.5%.

Unit 3   Test your knowledge

Activity I: Wrong or right answers

This is a quick test to help you check how much you have understood.

In the following statements, there are some right and some wrong answers. Circle only the wrong answer:

1   Costs are the money which a business:

   a   makes from selling its products.
   b   borrows from a bank or another business.
   c   spends in order to produce goods and services for its customers.

2   Fixed costs are costs which:

   a   remain unchanged at whatever the level of output the business is producing over a period of time.
   b   which change directly with the output of a business.
   c   an owner pays to start up the business.
   d   a business pays when it trades with suppliers or customers.

3   Profit is the money which is:

   a   paid to workers for doing their jobs.
   b   is left when all costs paid in making and selling a product are taken away from the revenue gained from that sale.
   c   made from selling a product.

4   Sales revenue is the money which a business:

   a   receives as a result of selling its products.
   b   pays for making and selling a product.
   c   receives from selling the products and after taking away all costs.

5   Variable costs are costs which:

   a   directly vary with the output of a business.
   b   don't change with the change in the level of production
   c   a business has to pay for making and selling a product

6   Running costs are costs which:

   a   a business pays on any non-trading expense.
   b   relate to a business's trading activities, including VAT.
   c   vary with the changes in the level of production.

7   A budget is:

   a   a statement which shows how much the business owes to others.
   b   an account which shows how much profit the business made last year.
   c   a plan showing the expected sales revenue and costs over the coming month or year.

8   Cash flow is the flow of money:

   a   into and out of a business.
   b   between suppliers and a business.
   c   between customers and a business.

9   A purchase order form is a form which:

   a   is sent from the supplier to the business (shop or warehouse) when an order is received.

b firms have to complete and send to the supplier to order or buy a product. It includes all the details about this product.

c includes a summary of transactions over a period of time. It shows records of payments and receipts.

10 A cheque is:

a the only method of payment for goods or services.

b an order written by the person who writes to the bank to pay on demand a specific sum of money to someone else.

c the quickest method of payment.

11 A cheque guarantee card is a card which:

a a retailer issues to guarantee the quality of a product.

b guarantees that the banks will honour the cheque.

c a bank issues to customers that guarantees the account will always have plenty of money.

12 A credit card is a card that is:

a used to pay for goods or services. It allows nearly six weeks for customers to pay for the goods.

b obtainable by anyone from a bank or building society.

c issued by a store or a retailer to customers to purchase goods.

13 The cost of new machinery and equipment is considered as:

a variable cost.
b fixed cost.
c start-up cost.

14 A credit note is a note that is:

a issued by a business to a customer. It entitles the buyer of the product to a full refund of the cost of returned items.

b carried by the driver of the delivery vehicle. It is a list of the products that have been sent by a supplier.

c completed when a petty cash purchase is made.

15 A receipt is:

a the customer's evidence of paying for the product, and it proves his/her ownership of the product.

b a document which is sent by a business at the same time as a statement of account.

c the order which is received by a business or supplier to check whether items are in stock and what price is to be charged.

16 The cost of renting business premises is considered as:

a start-up cost.
b running cost.
c variable cost.

Activity 2

Which financial document would you use in each of the following situations?

1 The manager of Speed Ltd asked you to order new machinery. You have to fill in and send a document to the supplier Engineering Manufacturing Ltd to order the new machinery. What is the document?

a   a cheque
b   a receipt
c   a purchase order form
d   an invoice.

2   Engineering Manufacturing Ltd send you a statement with:

a   an invoice
b   a purchase order form
c   statement of account
d   a cheque.

3   Your sales manager asked you to issue a document to a customer who purchased a faulty product to entitle her to a full refund of the cost of the returned CD player. What is the document?

a   a receipt
b   an invoice

c   a credit note
d   a petty cash voucher.

4   The administration manager of Speed Ltd asked you to record in a document the expenditure on milk. What is the document?

a   petty cash voucher
b   invoice
c   statement of account
d   remittance advice.

6   Your finance manager asked you to check if Engineering Manufacturing Ltd has sent a document to prove Speed Ltd's ownership of the new machinery. What is the document?

a   receipt
b   credit note
c   invoice
d   delivery note.

LIGHT DELIGHT ICE-CREAM LTD

Unit 28 Penraven Industrial Estate
Mean Wood Road
LEEDS
LS7 2AP

Tel. No.: 0113 234543 **Order** VAT Reg No: 680 73842 88

Date: 3/7/200

Order No. DF/1315

To:

Please supply

Quantity	Description	Ref	Unit Price

Delivery: asap
Signed by

LIGHT DELIGHT ICE-CREAM LTD

Unit 28 Penraven Industrial Estate
Mean Wood Road
LEEDS
LS7 2AP

DELIVERY NOTE

To   **VAT REG NO 680/7384288**

Your order	Invoice date	Invoice No	Dispatch date

Quantity	Description	Cat No

Received by.......   **Date:**

LIGHT DELIGHT ICE-CREAM LTD

Unit 28 Penraven Industrial Estate
Mean Wood Road
LEEDS
LS7 2AP

INVOICE

VAT REG NO 680/7384288

Customer

Customer Ref. No:
Despatch Date:

Invoice No:
Date

Quantity	Description	Unit Price	Total
	E&OE	Subtotal Discount 5% Amount after discount VAT (17.5%) Total	

LIGHT DELIGHT ICE-CREAM LTD

Unit 28 Penraven Industrial Estate
Mean Wood Road
LEEDS
LS7 2AP

FAX: 0113 234543   VAT REG NO 680/73842/88
TEL: 0113 234544

STATEMENT

To:

Date: Account no

Date	Details	Debit	Credit	Balance
Total outstanding balance				

REMITTANCE ADVICE

Ref No 2232

Please send payment to: Customer name:

LIGHT DELIGHT ICE-CREAM LTD

Unit 28 Penraven Industrial Estate
Mean Wood Road
LEEDS
LS7 2AP

Customer Account No: Cheque:...............................

Amount due: Cash:....................................

                                        Total amount paid ....

Petty cash voucher   **No**

                                Date:

For what required   **Amount**
                                £   P

Total Cash Spending

VAT is included
Signature   ---------------------------------------

Authorised   ---------------------------------------

LIGHT DELIGHT ICE-CREAM LTD

Unit 28 Penraven Industrial Estate
Mean Wood Road
LEEDS
LS7 2AP

RECEIPT   No

RECEIVED FROM: ....

....

.... £

the payment of ....

Received by .... Date ....

| Date _____ | ▼ The Royal Midshire | Date _____ 20 _ | **16-13-20** |

Date _____

_____

_____

_____

£ _____

265540

▼ The Royal Midshire Bank plc

Date _____ 20 _   **16-13-20**

or order

Pay _____

£

Light Delight

..·265540·16...1399:1 2890635..

Date _____

_____

_____

_____

£ _____

265541

▼ The Royal Midshire Bank plc

Date _____ 20 _   **16-13-20**

or order

Pay _____

£

Light Delight

..·265541·16...1399:1 2890635..

FAX MESSAGE

LIGHT DELIGHT ICE-CREAM LTD

Unit 28 Penraven Industrial Estate
Mean Wood Road
LEEDS
LS7 2AP

FAX NO: 0113 234543

TO:
DATE:

Ready to move on?

This is exactly what you need for the GNVQ Intermediate Business award

Choose from two student books

The *Student Book without Options* covers all of the compulsory units, making it ideal for a Part One GNVQ.

The *Student Book with Options* covers the compulsory units and four Edexcel option units: Individuals and the Organisation; Retailing; Consumer Protection; and Administrative Systems. It's ideal if you are taking the full award.

Learn about real businesses

'Snapshots' show you how real organisations apply the theory of business. Activities and case studies give you the opportunity to apply your knowledge to business situations.

Use the books easily

Chapters and sub-sections in the book match the headings in the GNVQ award specification, so it's easy to find your way around the text.

Index